Workbook for

Tonal Harmony

Workbook for

Tonal Harmony

with an Introduction to Twentieth-Century Music

Fifth Edition

Stefan Kostka
The University of Texas at Austin

Dorothy Payne
The University of South Carolina

Boston   Burr Ridge, IL   Dubuque, IA   Madison, WI   New York   San Francisco   St. Louis
Bangkok   Bogotá   Caracas   Kuala Lumpur   Lisbon   London   Madrid   Mexico City
Milan   Montreal   New Delhi   Santiago   Seoul   Singapore   Sydney   Taipei   Toronto

Contents

This icon denotes a listening example. For a list of the recorded examples, see the last page of the workbook.

EXERCISE 2-2

A. Fill in the blanks.

	Beat and meter type	Beat note	Division of the beat	Time signature
1.				𝄴
2.	Simple triple	𝅗𝅥		
3.	Simple duple		♫	
4.		♪		2
5.	Simple quadruple		♫	

B. Renotate the excerpts from Example 2-1 using the specified time signatures.

"Jingle Bells"

"America the Beautiful"

"Home on the Range"

EXERCISE 2-3

A. Fill in the blanks.

	Beat and meter type	*Beat note*	*Division of the beat*	*Time signature*
1.	Compound triple	♩.		
2.				6 16
3.			♪♪♪	12
4.	Compound duple		♩ ♩ ♩	
5.		♪.		9

B. Renotate the excerpts from Example 2-2 using the specified time signatures.

"Take Me Out to the Ball Game"

"Down in the Valley"

"Pop Goes the Weasel"

EXERCISE 2-4

A. Fill in the blanks.

	Beat and meter type	*Beat note*	*Division of the beat*	*Time signature*
1.	Compound quadruple		♪♪♪	
2.	Simple triple		♬	
3.			♪ ♪	4
4.		♪		6
5.				¢
6.			♪ ♪ ♪	9

B. Each measure below is incomplete. Add one or more rests to complete the measure.

1. $\frac{6}{4}$ 𝅗𝅥. ⌣ 𝅗𝅥. |

2. **C** 𝅗𝅥.. |

3. $\frac{2}{16}$ 𝅘𝅥𝅲 |

4. $\frac{12}{16}$ 𝅘𝅥. ♪ |

5. $\frac{3}{8}$ 𝅘𝅥𝅯 ♪ |

6. $\frac{9}{8}$ 𝅘𝅥𝅮𝅘𝅥𝅮𝅘𝅥𝅮 𝅘𝅥 |

7. **¢** 𝅗𝅥 ⌣ ♪. |

8. $\frac{9}{4}$ 𝅝. |

9. $\frac{3}{2}$ 𝅗𝅥 𝅘𝅥 𝅘𝅥 𝅘𝅥 |

10. $\frac{12}{8}$ 𝅘𝅥. 𝅘𝅥. 𝅘𝅥 |

11. $\frac{4}{8}$ 𝅘𝅥. |

12. $\frac{6}{4}$ 𝅘𝅥 𝅘𝅥 𝅘𝅥𝅘𝅥𝅘𝅥𝅘𝅥 𝅘𝅥 |

C. Provide the best time signature for each measure. In some cases more than one correct answer might be possible.

D. Each fragment below is notated so that the placement of the beats is obscured in some fashion. Without changing the way the music will sound, rewrite each one to clarify the beat placement.

E. Add stems as required.

1. Each duration is a half note.

2. Each duration is a sixteenth note. Beam them in groups of four.

F. Scale review. Fill in the key, scale degree, or note, whichever is missing. Assume the melodic minor form for all minor keys.

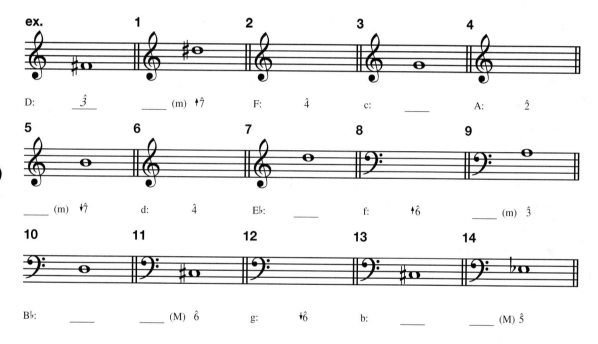

G. Interval review. Notate the specified interval above the given note.

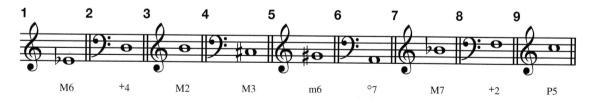

H. Interval review. Notate the specified interval below the given note.

EXERCISE 3-2

A. Identify the type of seventh chord, using the abbreviations given in Example 3-3.

B. Notate the seventh chord, given the root and type.

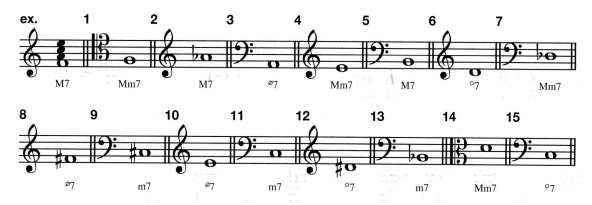

C. Given the seventh-chord quality and one member of the chord, notate the rest of the chord.

ex.   1   2   3   4   5   6   7

5th   7th   3rd   5th   5th   3rd   7th   root
m7   M7   m7   ⌀7   m7   Mm7   ⌀7   M7

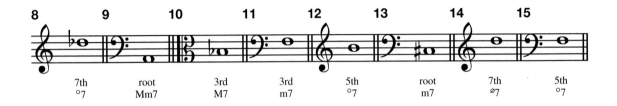

8   9   10   11   12   13   14   15

7th   root   3rd   3rd   5th   root   7th   5th
°7   Mm7   M7   m7   °7   m7   ⌀7   °7

EXERCISE 3-3

A. Identify the root and type of each chord and show the correct inversion symbol.

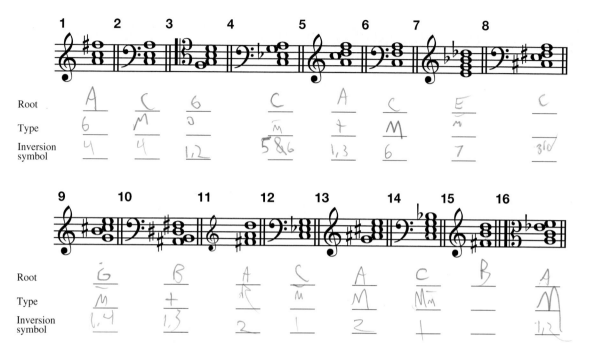

B. Fill in the blanks below each figured bass with the root and chord type that would be played at the corresponding point in the excerpt by using lead sheet symbols. The figures 5 and $\frac{5}{3}$ both mean to use a root position triad.

1. Bach, "Gott lebet noch" (adapted)

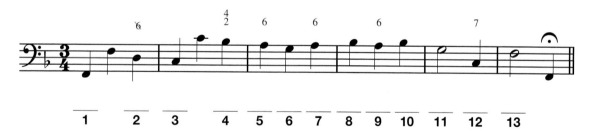

2. Bach, "Dich bet' ich an, mein höchster Gott"

(The first C♯3 in the bass is not to be harmonized.)

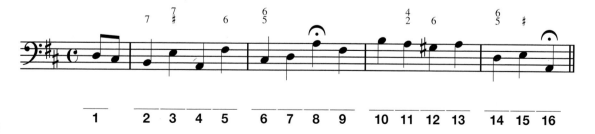

3.   Corelli, Sonata V, Op. 2, Sarabande

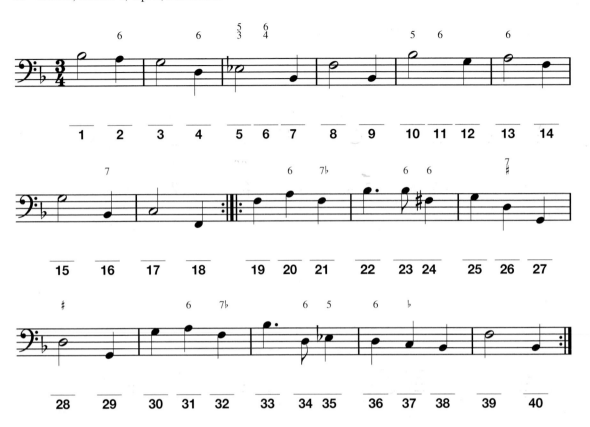

C.   Notate using half notes on the bottom staff the chords indicated by the lead sheet symbols. Notate all chords in root position.

Terry, "Serenade to a Bus Seat"

By Clark Terry. © 1958 (renewed 1986) Orpheum Music, Berkeley, CA.

EXERCISE 3-4

A. Identify the root and type of each chord and show the correct inversion symbol. All
the notes in each example belong to the same chord. The lowest note in each example
is the bass note for the purpose of analysis.

Root   ____   ____   ____   ____

Type   ____   ____   ____   ____

Inversion
symbol   ____   ____   ____   ____

Root   ____   ____   ____   ____   ____

Type   ____   ____   ____   ____   ____

Inversion
symbol   ____   ____   ____   ____   ____

B. The excerpts below are to be analyzed in a similar way. Each chord is numbered. Put
    your analysis of the chords in the blanks below the excerpt. Notes in parentheses
    should be ignored for the purposes of this exercise.

1. Bach, "Wer weiss, wie nahe mir mein Ende"

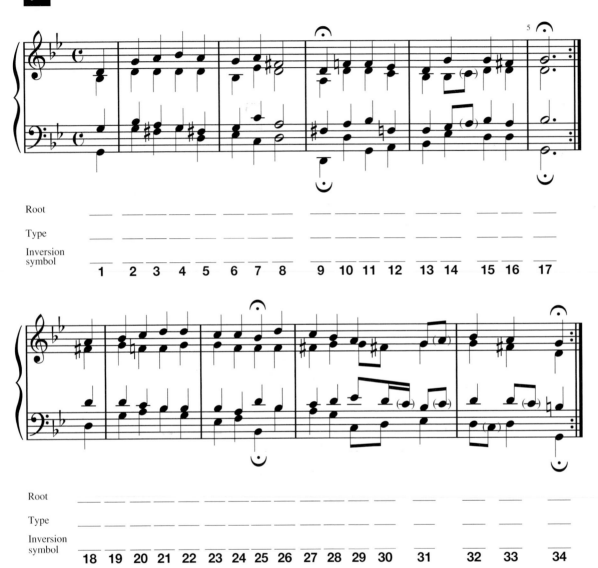

Root   _____ _____ _____ _____ _____ _____ _____ _____ _____ _____ _____ _____ _____ _____ _____ _____ _____

Type   _____ _____ _____ _____ _____ _____ _____ _____ _____ _____ _____ _____ _____ _____ _____ _____ _____

Inversion
symbol   _____ _____ _____ _____ _____ _____ _____ _____ _____ _____ _____ _____ _____ _____ _____ _____ _____
           1   2   3   4   5   6   7   8   9   10   11   12   13   14   15   16   17

Root   _____ _____ _____ _____ _____ _____ _____ _____ _____ _____ _____ _____ _____ _____ _____ _____

Type   _____ _____ _____ _____ _____ _____ _____ _____ _____ _____ _____ _____ _____ _____ _____ _____

Inversion
symbol   _____ _____ _____ _____ _____ _____ _____ _____ _____ _____ _____ _____ _____ _____ _____ _____
           18   19   20   21   22   23   24   25   26   27   28   29   30   31   32   33   34

2. Schumann, "Ich will meine Seele tauchen," Op. 48, No. 5

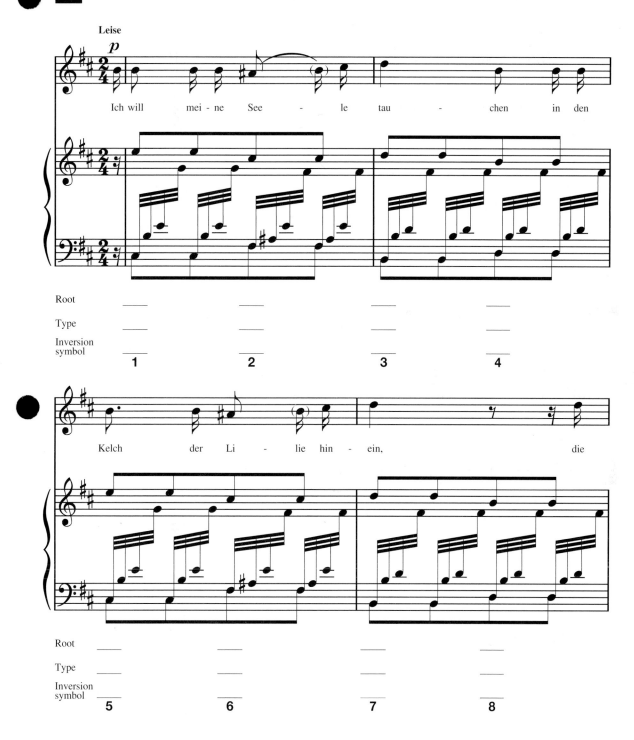

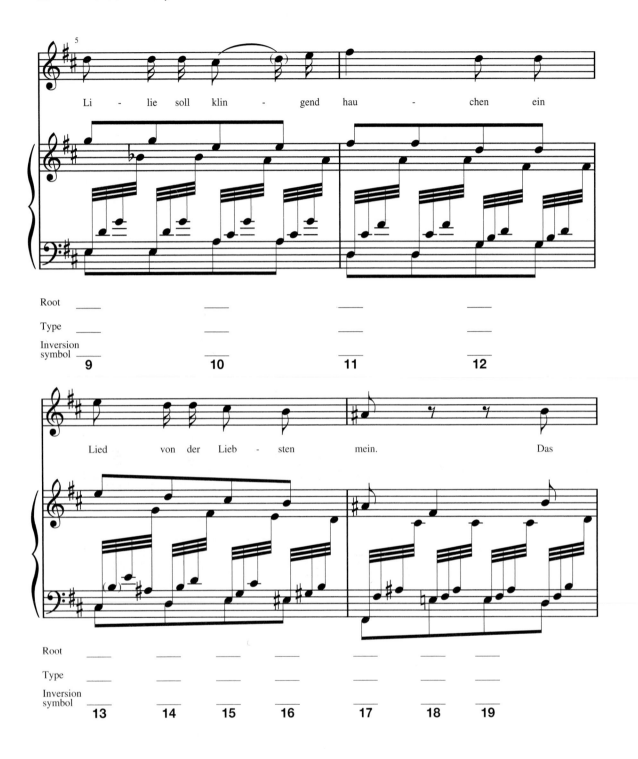

Li - lie soll klin - gend hau - chen ein

Root ____   ____   ____   ____

Type ____   ____   ____   ____

Inversion
symbol ____   ____   ____   ____

    9   **10**   **11**   **12**

Lied   von der Lieb - sten   mein.   Das

Root ____ ____ ____ ____   ____ ____ ____

Type ____ ____ ____ ____   ____ ____ ____

Inversion
symbol ____ ____ ____ ____   ____ ____ ____

   13 **14** **15** **16**   **17** **18** **19**

3. Gottschalk, "Jerusalem"

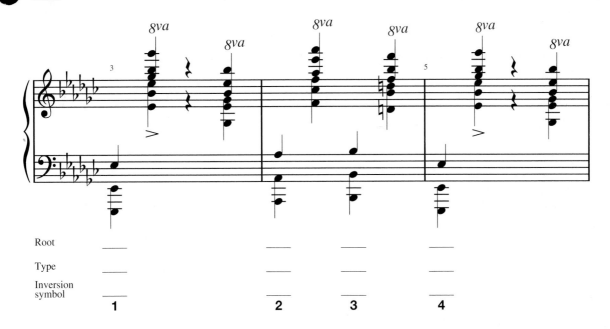

Root   _____   _____   _____   _____

Type   _____   _____   _____   _____

Inversion
symbol   _____   _____   _____   _____

     1   **2**   **3**   **4**

Root   _____   _____   _____   _____   _____

Type   _____   _____   _____   _____   _____

Inversion
symbol   _____   _____   _____   _____   _____

     5   **6**   **7**   **8**   **9**

Chapter 4

DIATONIC CHORDS IN MAJOR AND MINOR KEYS

EXERCISE 4-1

A. Given the key and the triad, supply the roman numeral. Be sure your roman numeral is of the correct type (uppercase or lowercase). Inversion symbols, where required, go to the upper right of the roman numeral (as in I⁶).

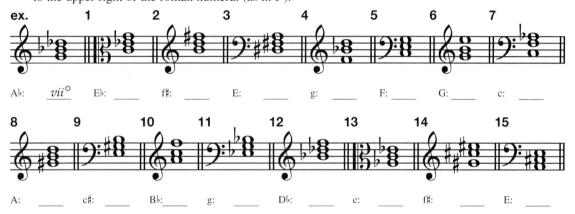

B. In the exercise below you are given the name of a key and a scale degree number (in parentheses). *Without using key signatures*, notate the triad on that scale degree and provide the roman numeral. In minor keys be sure to use the triad types circled in Example 4-7 (p. 61).

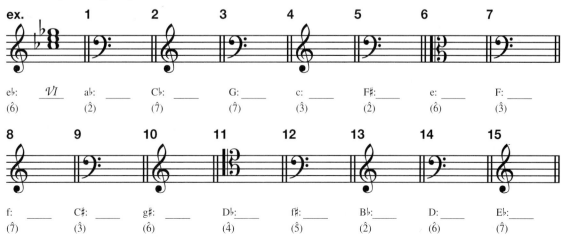

C. Analysis. Write roman numerals in the spaces provided, making sure each roman numeral is of the correct type and includes an inversion symbol if necessary.

1.   Handel, "Wenn mein Stündlein vorhanden ist"

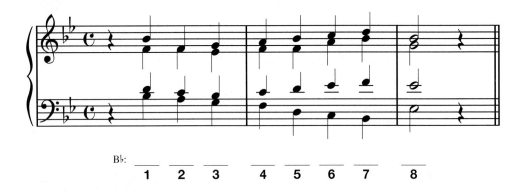

B♭: ___ ___ ___   ___ ___ ___ ___   ___
    1   2   3   4   5   6   7   8

2.   Handel, "Wenn mein Stündlein vorhanden ist"

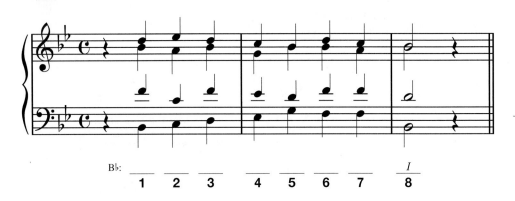

B♭: ___ ___ ___   ___ ___ ___ ___   *I*
                                     ___
    1   2   3   4   5   6   7   8

D. Fill in the blanks, using the example as a model.

	Key	This chord	Has this bass note
ex.	C	I^6	E
1.	a	V^6	
2.		IV^6	C
3.	c♯	ii^{o6}	
4.	B	$^6_4$	C♯
5.		i^6_4	D
6.	F	vii^{o6}	

EXERCISE 4-2

A. Given the key and the seventh chord, provide the roman numeral. Be sure your roman numeral is the correct type and includes an inversion symbol if necessary.

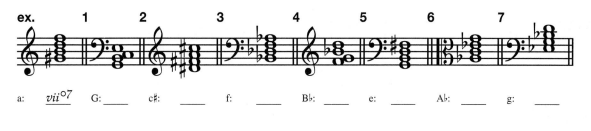

a: *vii°7*   G: ____   c#: ____   f: ____   Bb: ____   e: ____   Ab: ____   g: ____

d: ____   E: ____   F: ____   A: ____   Eb: ____   b: ____   c: ____   D: ____

B. In the exercises below you are given the name of a key and a scale degree number (in parentheses). Without using key signatures, notate the seventh chord on that scale degree in root position and provide the roman numeral. In minor keys, be sure to use the chord types shown in Example 4-9 (p. 65).

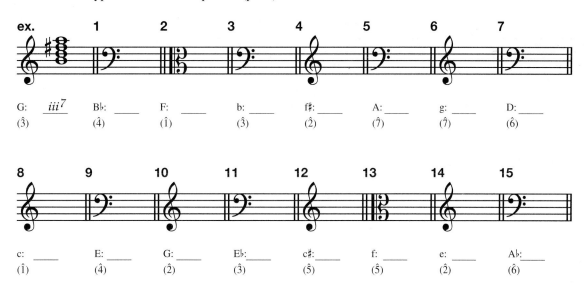

G: *iii7*   Bb: ____   F: ____   b: ____   f#: ____   A: ____   g: ____   D: ____
(3̂)   (4̂)   (1̂)   (3̂)   (2̂)   (7̂)   (7̂)   (6̂)

c: ____   E: ____   G: ____   Eb: ____   c#: ____   f: ____   e: ____   Ab: ____
(1̂)   (4̂)   (2̂)   (3̂)   (5̂)   (5̂)   (2̂)   (6̂)

C. Analysis. Put roman numerals in the spaces provided, making sure each roman numeral is of the correct type and includes an inversion symbol, if needed.

1. Beethoven, "Variations on a Theme" by Paisiello

2. Brahms, "Minnelied," Op. 44, No. 1

Chapter 5

PRINCIPLES OF VOICE LEADING

EXERCISE 5-1

A. Criticize each melody in terms of the rules for simple melodies discussed on pages 71–72.

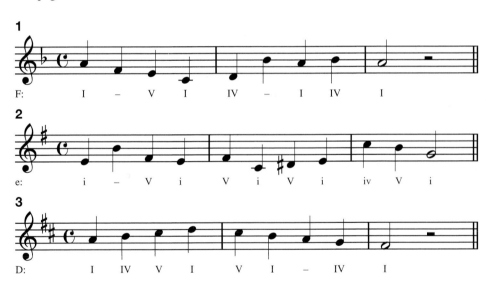

B. Compose simple melodies that will conform to these progressions.

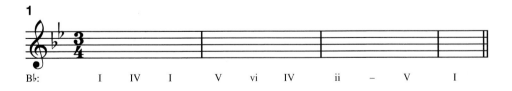

2

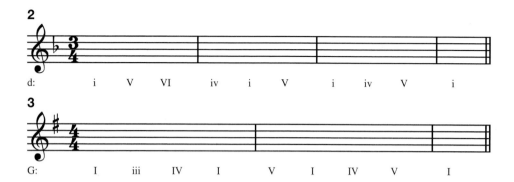

d: i   V   VI   iv   i   V   i   iv   V   i

3

G: I   iii   IV   I   V   I   IV   V   I

EXERCISE 5-2

A. Analyze the excerpt below, using roman numerals. Then show beneath each roman
    numeral the structure of the chord by writing "C" or "O" for close or open structure.
    The notes in parentheses are not part of the chord and should be ignored for the pur-
    pose of harmonic analysis.

Schumann, "Roundelay," Op. 68, No. 22

A: ___   ___ ___   ___ ___ ___ V^7 ___

B. Review the two conventions concerning spacing on pages 74–75. Then point out in the
    example below any places where those conventions are not followed.

C. Fill in the circled missing inner voice(s) to complete each root position triad, being sure that each note of the triad is represented. Follow the spacing conventions and stay within the range of each vocal part.

D. In the examples below you are given the soprano note for each chord. Supply the alto, tenor, and bass notes to complete the specified triad in close or open position, as indicated. Be sure to double the root of each chord and to follow the spacing conventions.

EXERCISE 5-3

A. Label the chords in the excerpt below with roman numerals. Then label any examples of parallelism (objectionable or otherwise) that you can find.

Bach, "Ermuntre dich, mein schwacher Geist"

B. Find and label the following errors in this passage:

1. Parallel 8ves

2. Parallel 5ths

3. Direct 5th

4. Consecutive 5ths by contrary motion

5. Spacing error (review pp. 74–75)

C. Find and label the following errors in this passage:

1. Parallel 8ves

2. Parallel 5ths

3. Direct 8ve

4. Spacing error

Chapter 6

ROOT POSITION PART WRITING

EXERCISE 6-1. *Using repeated triads*

Fill in the inner voice or voices in the second chord of each exercise. The key is F major throughout. Double the roots of the triads in the four-voice examples.

1 four parts

2 three parts

EXERCISE 6-2.   *Using roots a 4th (5th) apart*

A. Add alto and tenor parts to each exercise below. Each progression involves roots a P4
    (P5) apart. Use one of the three methods outlined on pages 87–88 in each case and
    state which you have used.

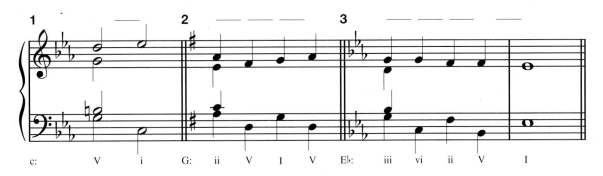

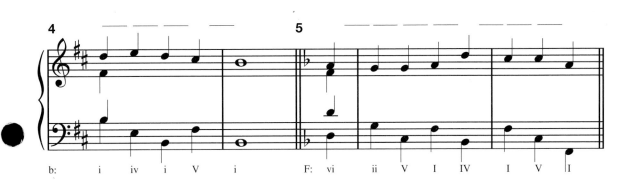

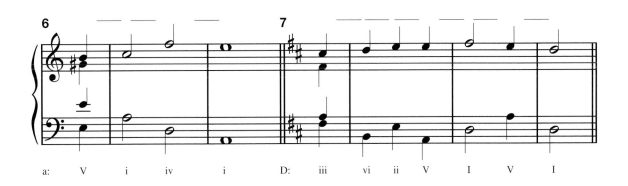

B. Add an alto part to each exercise. Be careful to observe conventions concerning spacing, parallels, and doubling. Each triad should include at least a root and a 3rd.

F: ii   V   I   IV   I   f#:   i   V   i   iv   A: iii   vi   ii   V   I

EXERCISE 6-3.   *Using roots a 4th (5th) and 3rd (6th) apart*

A.   Add alto and tenor parts to each exercise below. Use the smoothest voice leading in
each case. For roots a 4th (5th) apart, state which method you have used.

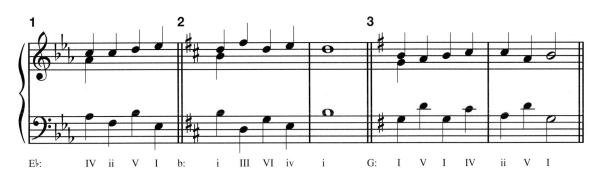

B.   Add an alto part to each exercise below. Be careful to observe the conventions concerning parallels, spacing, and doubling.

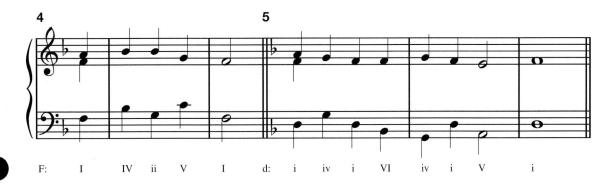

EXERCISE 6-4.   *Using all root relationships*

A. Complete each progression. Make two versions of each: one for three parts (adding an alto) and one for four parts (adding alto and tenor). In the four-part versions, state which method you have used for any progression by 4th or 5th.

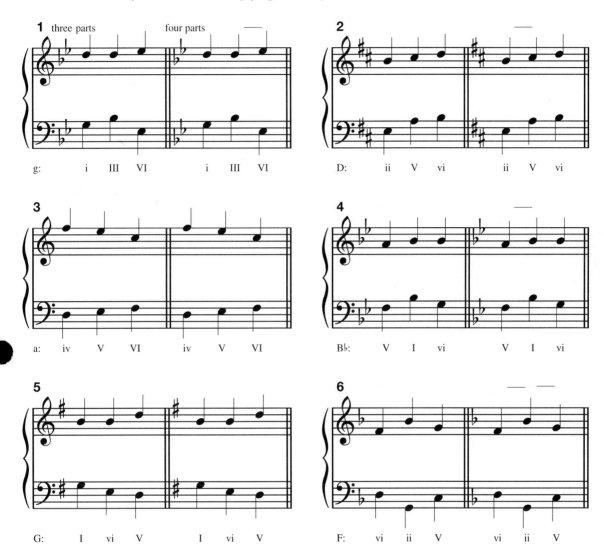

B.   Fill in alto and tenor parts in these exercises.

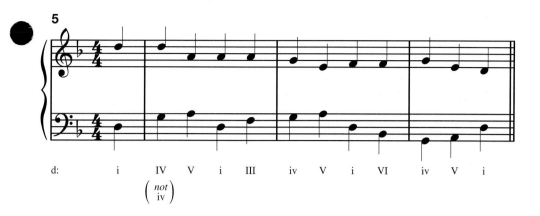

d: i   IV   V   i   III   iv   V   i   VI   iv   V   i

$\left(\begin{array}{c} not \\ iv \end{array}\right)$

C. Name the keys and analyze the chords specified by these figured basses. Then compose a good melody line for each. Finally, fill in alto and tenor parts to make a four-part texture.

D. Write the following short progressions in root position for combinations of three and four parts.

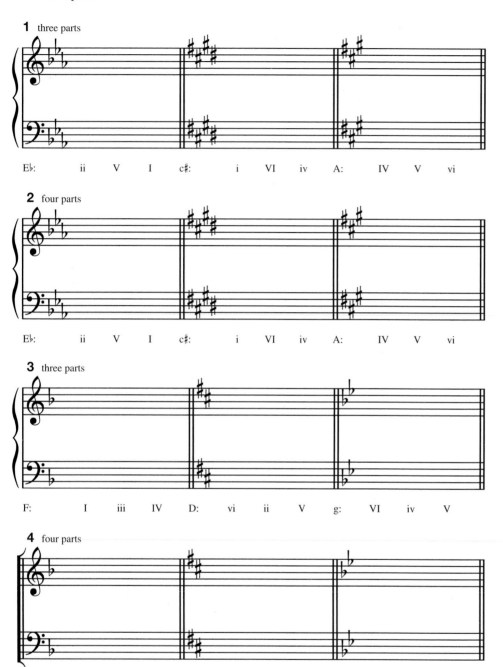

1 three parts

Eb: ii   V   I   c#:   i   VI   iv   A: IV   V   vi

2 four parts

Eb: ii   V   I   c#:   i   VI   iv   A: IV   V   vi

3 three parts

F: I   iii   IV   D: vi   ii   V   g: VI   iv   V

4 four parts

F: I   iii   IV   D: vi   ii   V   g: VI   iv   V

EXERCISE 6-5

A. Notate the chords below for the specified instruments. Each chord is written at con-
    cert pitch, so transpose as needed for the performers. Use the correct clef for each
    instrument. Note that the instruments are listed in score order, the order used in
    Appendix A, which is not always the same as order by pitch.

Fl.	Ob.	Clar. in B♭	Bsn.	A. Sax
T. Sax.	Hn. in F	Tpt. in B♭	Trb.	Hn. in F
Vla.	Vl.	Vc.	D.B.	Tuba

B. Set the following progression for combinations of three and four parts. If possible, score for instruments in your class. Use root position only.

1 three parts (reduced score)

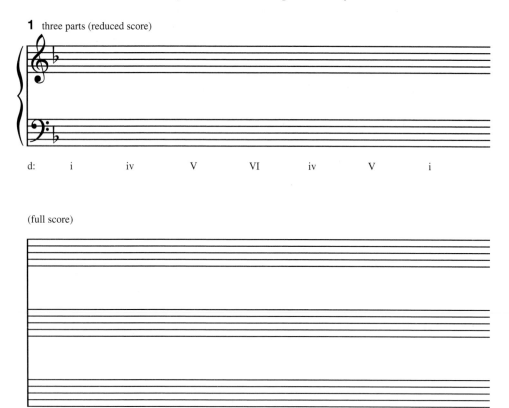

d: i   iv   V   VI   iv   V   i

(full score)

2 four parts (reduced score)

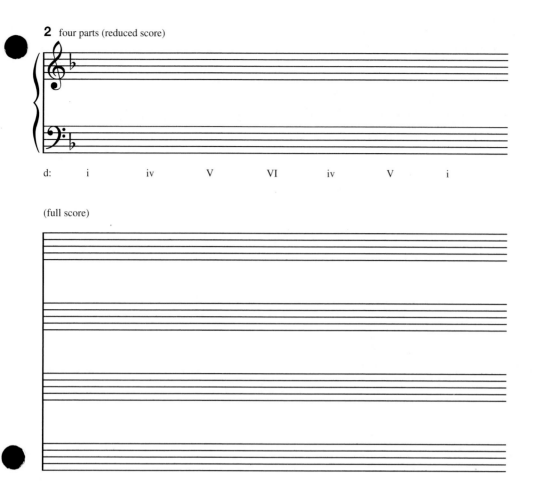

d: i   iv   V   VI   iv   V   i

(full score)

C. Write a version of the excerpt below on a grand staff by transposing the parts to concert pitch. Play your version on the piano and analyze the harmonies if you can.

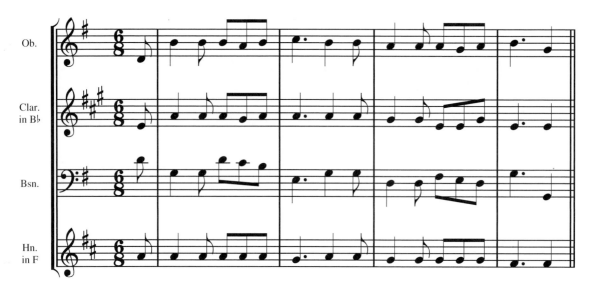

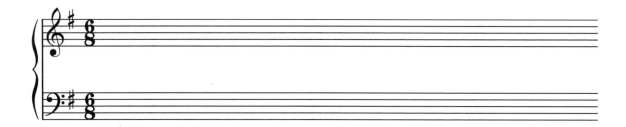

Chapter 7

HARMONIC PROGRESSION

EXERCISE 7-1

A. Complete each progression to conform with the chord diagrams on pages 103–109.
    The chord in the blank should be different from those on either side of it. In most
    cases, there is more than one correct answer.

    1. IV   _?_   I   (____ or ____)   **4.** iii   _?_   V   (____)

    2. vi   _?_   I   (____)   **5.** vii°   _?_   vi   (____)

    3. I   _?_   ii   (____ or ____)   **6.** vi   _?_   ii   (____)

B. Bracket any portions of these progressions that do not conform to the chord diagrams
    on pages 103–109.

    1. i   vii°   i   iv   VI   V   i

    2. I   vi   ii   IV   I   V   I

    3. I   iii   IV   vii°   I   IV   V   I

    4. i   III   iv   i   iv   V   vii°   i

C. Analysis. Label all chords with roman numerals and bracket any successions of
    chords that do not agree with the chord diagrams on pages 103–109.

    1. Bach, "Du Friedensfürst, Herr Jesu Christ"

2. Vivaldi, Cello Sonata in G Minor, Prelude. Unfigured bass realization by
S. Kostka.

Non-chord tones in the solo part have not been put in parentheses, but the
harmonic analysis can be done by concentrating on the accompaniment. The
key is g minor, despite what appears to be an incorrect key signature. Key
signatures had not yet become standardized when this work was composed.

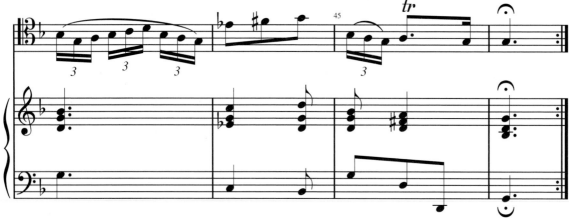

D. Analyze the chords specified by these figured basses and add inner voices to make a four-part texture. Bracket all circle-of-fifths progressions, even those that contain only two chords. Before beginning, review the partwriting for deceptive progressions.

1

2

3

E.   Analyze this figured bass, then add a good soprano line and inner voices. Bracket all circle-of-fifths progressions.

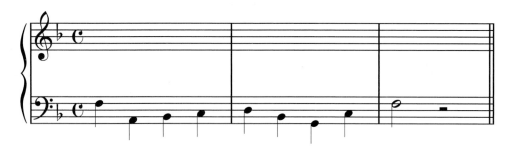

F.   Add an alto part (only) to mm. 1 to 2. Then compose a good soprano line for mm. 3 to 4 and fill in an alto part.

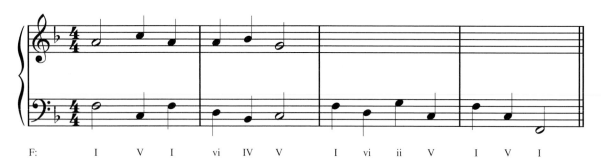

F: I   V   I   vi   IV   V   I   vi   ii   V   I   V   I

G.   Below are two unfigured bass lines. Using triads in root position and first inversion *only,* show a good harmonization of each one by placing roman numerals beneath the bass line. Be sure to refer to the diagrams on p. 109 while you work on your harmonizations.

1

2

H. Harmonize the melodies below by using root position major or minor (not diminished) triads in an acceptable progression. Try to give the bass a good contour while avoiding parallel and direct 5ths and 8ves with the melody. Be sure to include analysis. Finally, add one or two inner parts to make a version for SAB three-part chorus or SATB four-part chorus, as indicated.

1 SATB

G:

2 SAB

D:
or b:

3 SATB

E♭:

4 SAB

d:

5 SATB

E:

I.   Compose a *simple* melody, then follow the instructions for Part H. You might need to revise the melody as you work on the harmonization.

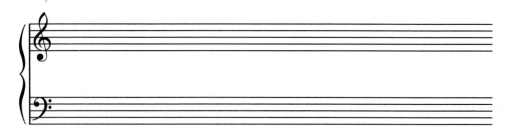

J.   Review: Label the chords with roman numerals and inversion symbols (where needed).

c: *iv⁶*   f: ____   Bb: ____   G: ____   d: ____   b: ____   E: ____   Ab: ____

f#: ____   g: ____   Eb: ____   D: ____   e: ____   c#: ____   F: ____   A: ____

Chapter 8

TRIADS IN FIRST INVERSION

EXERCISE 8-1

A. Analysis.

1. Bracket the longest series of parallel sixth chords (triads in first inversion) that you can find in this excerpt. Do not attempt a roman numeral analysis. Does the voice leading in the sixth-chord passage resemble more closely Example 8-8 (p. 121) or Example 8-9 (p. 122)?

Beethoven, Sonata Op. 2, No. 1, III

2. Label all chords with roman numerals. Then classify the doubling in each inverted triad according to the methods shown in Example 8-10 (p. 123).

Bach, "Was frag' ich nach der Welt"

3. Label all chords with roman numerals. Bracket the circle-of-fifths progression (review pp. 101–102).

Handel, Passacaglia

B. The excerpt below is from Mozart's String Quartet K. 428. Supply the missing tenor line (viola in the original).

C. Supply alto and tenor lines for the following passages.

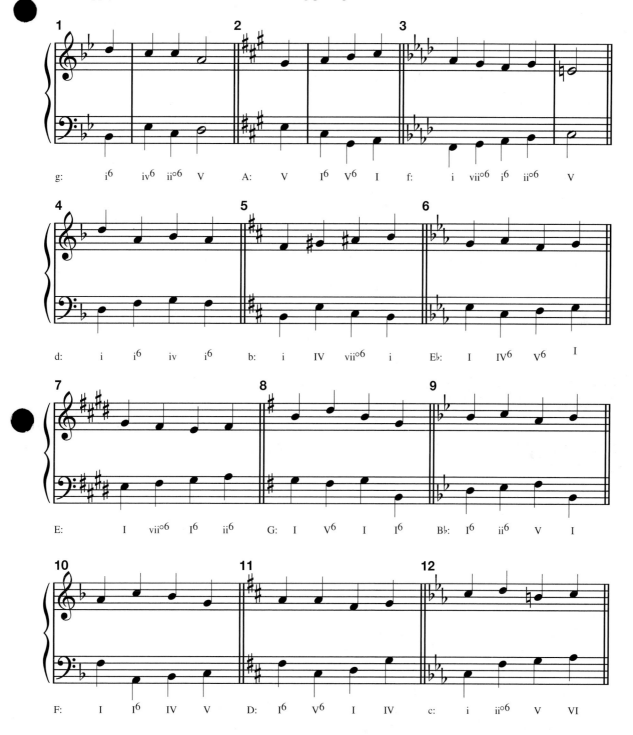

D. Supply alto lines for the following passages.

g: i⁶   iv⁶ ii°⁶ V   A: V   I⁶ V⁶   I   f: i   vii°⁶ i⁶ ii°⁶   V

d: i   i⁶   iv   i⁶   b: i   IV   vii°⁶   i   E♭:   I   IV⁶   V⁶   I

E. Analyze the harmonies implied by the soprano/bass lines below and add one or two
    inner parts, as specified by your instructor.

F:

e:

F. The following passage is reduced from Beethoven's Sonata Op. 10, No. 3, III. Analyze
    the implied harmonies (more than one good solution is possible) and add an alto line
    (only). Use only triads in root position and first inversion.

G. Continue your solution to Part D with a second eight-measure segment. The second
    part should be similar to the first, but if it starts exactly like it, objectionable parallels
    will result. Maintain the three-part texture.

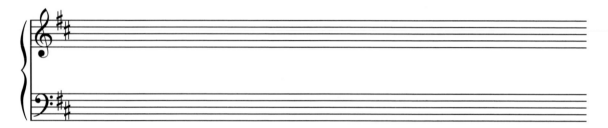

H. Review the figured bass information on pages 45–46. Then realize the figured basses
    below by following these steps:

    a. Provide the roman numerals specified by the figured bass.

    b. Compose a simple melody that will conform to the progression and at the same
       time will create a good counterpoint with the bass.

    c. Make two completed versions of each, one for three parts and one for four parts.

1 Three parts

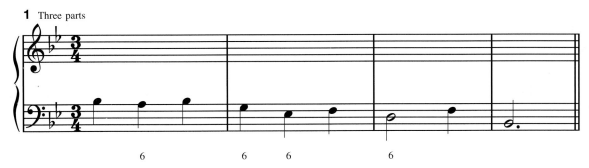

Bb:

Four parts

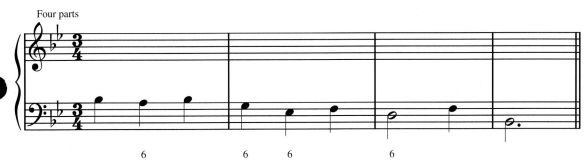

Bb:

2 Three parts (The horizontal line beneath the last measure means that the 3rd above the bass should be retained in the next chord.).

e:

Four parts

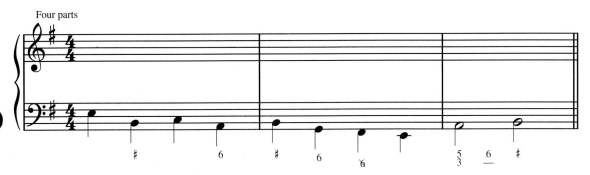

e:

I. Review the chord diagrams on pages 103–109. Then assign roman numerals to each of the bass notes in the exercises below, using triads (only) in root position and first inversion to create a good tonal progression. Then follow steps b and c for Part H. If possible these settings should be for vocal or instrumental combinations found in your class.

J.   Select roman numerals with which to harmonize this melody, changing chords every place there is a blank. Be sure your progression is a good one. Then write out the melody with a bass line, using first inversion triads where appropriate. Make sure that the bass creates a good counterpoint with the melody and that there are no objectionable parallels. Finally, make a piano setting, using the bass line you composed. Keep the piano texture simple, perhaps like that in Example 8-3 (p. 118).

Chapter 9

TRIADS IN SECOND INVERSION

EXERCISE 9-1

A. Analysis. In addition to the specific instructions for each example, label each six-four chord by type.

1. Label all chords with roman numerals.

Schumann, "The Wild Rider," Op. 68, No. 8

2. Label chords with roman numerals.

Handel, "Wenn mein Stündlein vorhanden ist"

3. Label the chords with roman numerals and put parentheses around all non-chord tones.

Clara Wieck Schumann, Scherzo, Op. 15, No. 4

Published 1976 by Willy Müller-Süddeutscher Verlag and 1994 by Breitkopf & Härtel.

4. In this excerpt, six-four chords are formed by arpeggiations in m. 1 and by a melodic bass in m. 2 (the bass in mm. 2–3 imitates the soprano melody in mm. 1–2). Put roman numerals in the blanks provided and put parentheses around all non-chord tones. Then show where any six-four chords occur, no matter how briefly.

Bach, English Suite No. 2, Courante

5. Label the chords with roman numerals. As before, identify the type of any six-four chord you encounter.

Haydn, Symphony No. 100, I

6. Label the chords with roman numerals, and identify the type of any six-four chord you encounter.

Beethoven, Piano Concerto No. 1, Op. 15, I

B. Fill in one or two inner parts, as specified. Identify any six-four chords by type.

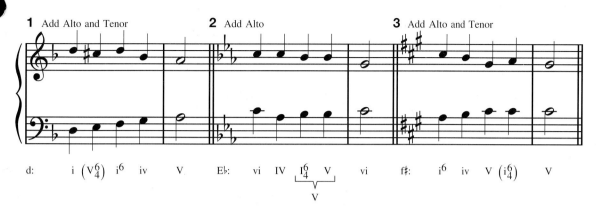

d: i $\left(V^6_4\right)$ i^6 iv   V   E♭:   vi   IV I^6_4 V   vi   f♯: i^6 iv   V $\left(i^6_4\right)$ V
                                                                    V

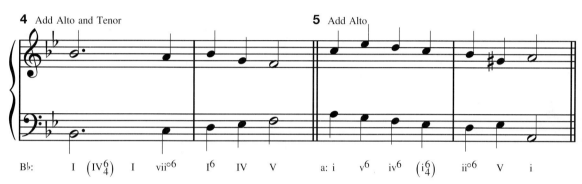

B♭:   I $\left(IV^6_4\right)$ I vii^{o6} I^6 IV   V   a: i v^6 iv^6 $\left(i^6_4\right)$ ii^{o6} V   i

C. Realize these figured basses for three or four voices, as specified, striving to create
    good outer-voice counterpoint. Notice the frequent use of $^5_3$ (or the equivalent, such
    as $^5_♯$) to indicate root-position triads following an inverted chord. Analyze with roman
    numerals and label six-four types.

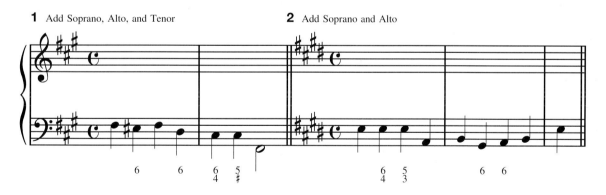

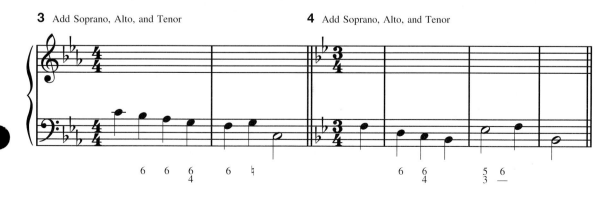

D. Harmonize each unfigured bass with a good tonal progression. Then compose a soprano line that will both fit the progression and create a good outer-voice counterpoint with the bass. Finally, fill in alto and tenor parts to make a four-part texture. Be sure to include a six-four chord in each one and identify the six-four type.

1

2

E. Harmonize each melody by composing a bass line that will create a good counterpoint with the melody and that will imply a good harmonic progression. Complete the harmonization by filling in two inner parts. Try to include an appropriate six-four chord in each harmonization.

1

G:

2

f:

F. Continue the accompaniment of this violin melody. Non-chord tones are in parentheses. Be sure to use at least one cadential, passing, or pedal six-four chord. Include a
harmonic analysis.

Chapter 10

CADENCES, PHRASES, AND PERIODS

EXERCISE 10-1

A. Cadences. Using only triads in root position and first inversion, compose examples of the following cadences. Each example should include three chords—the two cadence chords plus one chord preceding the cadence chords. Include key signatures and roman numerals.

1 three parts   **2** four parts   **3** three parts   **4** four parts

A: ____ ____ ____   g: ____ ____ ____   F: ____ ____ ____   b: ____ ____ ____

(root position IAC)   (DC—careful!)   (HC)   (inverted IAC)

5 three parts   **6** four parts   **7** three parts   **8** four parts

G: ____ ____ ____   d: ____ ____ ____   B♭: ____ ____ ____   e: ____ ____ ____

(PAC)   (PC)   (leading-tone IAC)   (Phrygian HC)

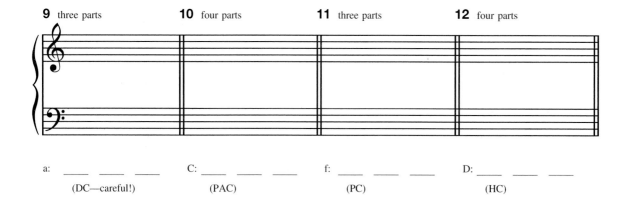

9 three parts   **10** four parts   **11** three parts   **12** four parts

a: ____ ____ ____   C: ____ ____ ____   f: ____ ____ ____   D: ____ ____ ____

(DC—careful!)   (PAC)   (PC)   (HC)

B.   Analysis. The cadence chords have been analyzed for you in each example. Make a
     diagram of each excerpt similar to the diagrams used in the text. Include phrase labels
     (a, b, and so on), cadence types and measures, and the form of the example.

   1.   Be sure to listen to this stirring theme in its original orchestral version as well.

       Schumann, Symphony No. 1, Op. 38, III (piano reduction)

2. Diagram and name the form of this excerpt. Also:

 a. Bracket all sequences in the melody.

 b. Find the best example of imitation between the melody and the bass.

 c. Label the chords implied by the two voices. Non-chord tones are in parentheses in the bass (only). Note: The best choice for m. 5 is *not* a ii chord. (Compare m. 5 with m. 13.)

Anonymous: Minuet in G, from the *Notebook for Anna Magdalena Bach*

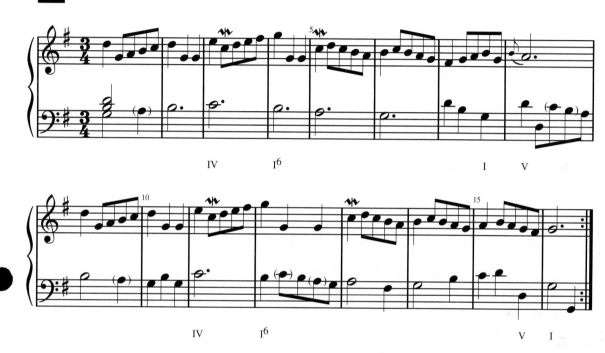

3. Do the two phrases here begin with similar material? Compare mm. 9 to 10 with mm. 13 to 14. Diagram and name the form.

Mozart, Violin Sonata K. 377, III

V⁷   I

4. Diagram and name the form of this excerpt, and copy out any rhythmic motives found in both of the phrases. The progression at *x* resembles an IAC in what key? What is the relationship between that key and e minor?

♫   Mendelssohn, *Song without Words,* Op. 62, No. 3

5. This excerpt is in the form of a three-phrase period (some would call it a phrase group). Would it be better to say that it has two antecedent phrases or two consequent phrases? Why? Which phrase features a circle-of-fifths sequence? Analyze all the chords in that phrase and diagram the form of the excerpt.

Mozart, Sonata K. 545, I

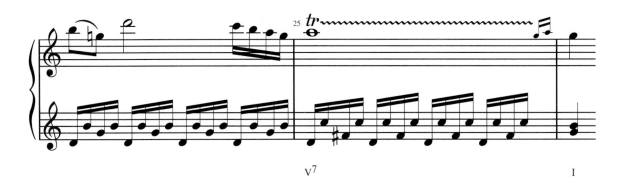

V⁷ ~~V⁷~~

I

6. Diagram the form of this excerpt in four ways, all of which are possible interpretations:
   (1) all four-measure phrases: 4+4+4+4+4; (2) four phrases, the last one extended:
   4+4+4+8; (3) two long phrases plus a short final phrase: 8+8+4; and (4) two phrases,
   the second extended: 8+12. Which interpretation do you prefer? Why?

Mozart, Sonata K. 310, III

7. Diagram and name the form of this theme, then label the first five chords. Also, see if you can find a disguised sequence hidden in the soprano and another in the bass in mm. 1 to 8.

Beethoven, Sonata Op. 13, II

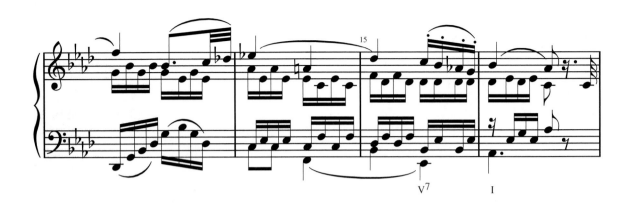

C. Review. Notate the chords in the keys and bass positions indicated.

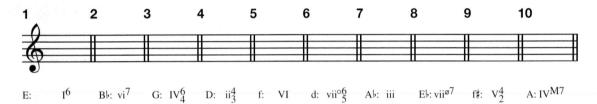

E: I^6 B♭: vi^7 G: IV^6_4 D: ii^4_3 f: VI d: vii^{o6}_5 A♭: iii E♭: $vii^{ø7}$ f♯: V^4_2 A: IV^{M7}

Chapter 11

NON-CHORD TONES 1

EXERCISE 11-1

A. Analysis.

1. Go back to Example 8-19 (p. 128), which shows NCTs in parentheses, and identify in the blanks below the type of each NCT found in the solo horn part. Always show the interval classification (4-3 and so on) when you analyze suspensions.

   m. 6 _____   m. 7 _____   _____   m. 8 _____   _____

   m. 10 _____   m. 11 _____   _____

2. Analyze the chords and NCTs in this excerpt. Then make a reduction similar to those seen in the text by (1) removing all NCTs, (2) using longer note values or ties for repeated notes, and (3) transposing parts by a P8 where necessary to make the lines smoother. Study the simplified texture. Do any voice-leading problems appear to have been covered up by the embellishments? Discuss the reasons for the leap in the tenor in m. 3.

   Bach, "Hilf, Herr Jesu, lass gelingen"

Reduction

B. After reviewing pages 172–176, decide what *one* suspension would be best in each excerpt below. Then renotate with the suspension and at least one other embellishment. Remember to put parentheses around NCTs and to label NCTs and arpeggiations.

b: V⁶   i ii°⁶   V   A: IV⁶ I   V   I⁶   g: i   iv   i⁶ vii°⁶   E♭:   IV V⁶   I   V⁶

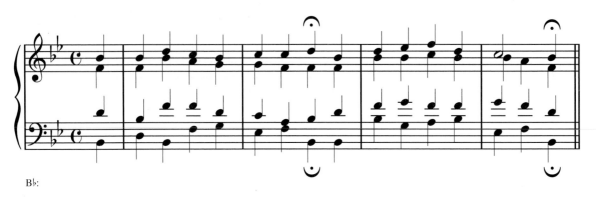

C. The example below is a simplified excerpt from a Bach chorale harmonization. Label the chords with roman numerals and activate the texture with stepwise NCTs, including at least one suspension. Label all embellishments.

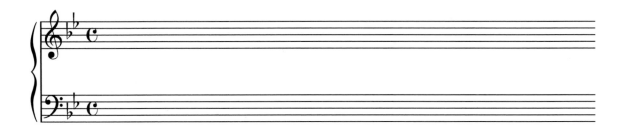

B♭:

D. In the figured basses below, the symbols "4 ♯" call for a 4-3 suspension, with a sharp
    applied to the note of resolution. The symbols "6 –" indicate that a first inversion triad
    is to be used above both C's in the bass.

For each figured bass, do the following:

1. Analyze the harmonies with roman numerals.

2. Compose a simple but musical soprano line.

3. Fill in one or two inner parts, as specified.

4. Add some stepwise NCTs to each example and label them.

1

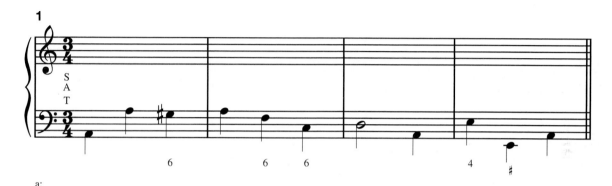

a:

2

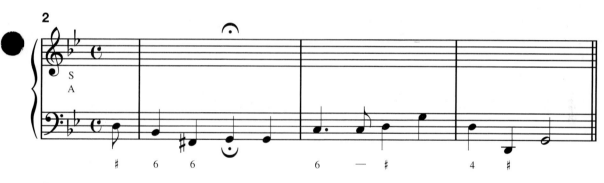

g:

E. Using the following progressions, compose a good soprano/bass framework, using inversions where desired. Next add one or two inner parts, as specified. Show with an *x* every possible location for a 9-8, 7-6, 4-3, or 2-3 suspension. Finally, create an elaborated version of the simple texture, including at least one suspension. Other embellishments should be limited to arpeggiations and stepwise NCTs.

1.   Three-part texture. (Remember that diminished triads should be used in first inversion.)

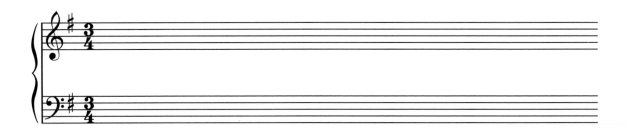

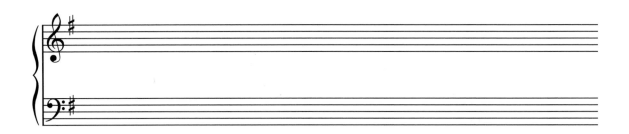

2. Four-part texture.

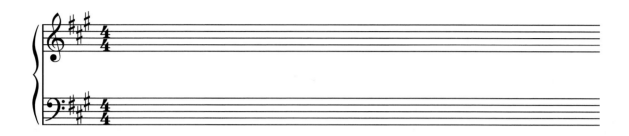

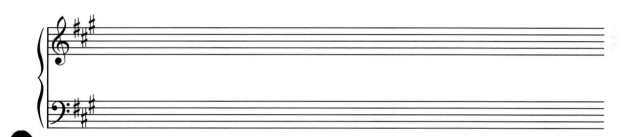

F. Compose your own harmonic progression and follow the instructions for part E. Try a two-, three-, or four-part texture.

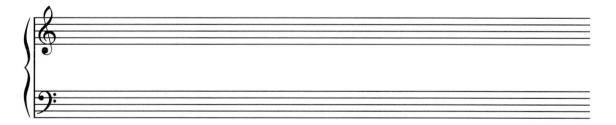

G. Analyze the chords implied by this two-voice framework. Then embellish the frame-
    work in an arrangement for string quartet. A suggested beginning is given.

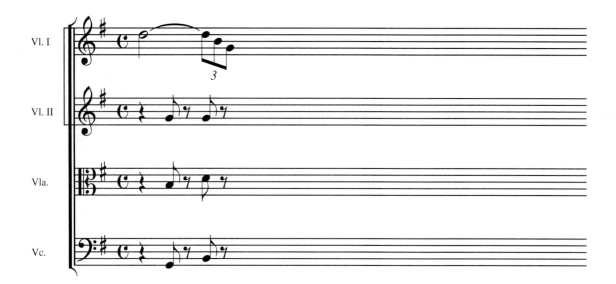

H. Continue your solution to Part G to form a parallel period.

Chapter 12

NON-CHORD TONES 2

EXERCISE 12-1

A. Analysis.

    1. Go back to Example 7-18 on page 108 of the text, where NCTs are shown in parentheses, and identify the type of each NCT in the blanks below. Always show the interval classification (7-6 and so on) when you analyze suspensions.

        m. 1 _____ _____   m. 3 _____ _____

    2. Do the same for Example 10-14 on page 158 of the text.

        m. 10 _____   m. 11 _____   m. 13 _____

        m. 14 _____   m. 15 _____   m. 16, violin: _____   piano: _____ _____

    3. Do the same for Example 9-12 on page 142.

        VI. I: m. 23 _____   m. 24 _____   m. 25 _____   m. 26 _____

        VI. II: m. 23 _____   m. 26 _____ _____ _____

    4. Label chords and NCTs in this excerpt.

Mozart, Piano Sonata, K. 545, II

G: _____

5. The chords in this excerpt have been labeled for you. Put parentheses around all NCTs in mm. 1 to 6 (only) and label them. The roman numerals in parentheses are part of a "nonfunctional" series of parallel sixth chords (review pp. 120–122), and some other chords have been left unlabeled because they are too advanced for you at this point. The last three measures are included for context, but they are not part of this exercise.

Clara Wieck Schumann, Larghetto, Op. 15, No. 1

Published 1976 by Willy Müller-Süddeutscher Verlag and 1994 by Breitkopf & Härtel.

6. The chords in this excerpt have been analyzed using lead sheet symbols. Put parentheses around all NCTs and label them.

Brahms, Intermezzo, Op. 76, No. 7

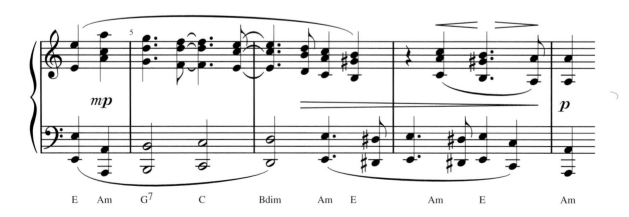

B.   Using a three-part texture, write authentic cadences in five different keys, employing
     a different NCT from the following list in each cadence: p, n, ant, app, e.

C.   Analyze the chords in this phrase with roman numerals. Then renotate the phrase on
     the staves below, adding at least 4 NCTs, at least 2 of which should be suspensions.
     Label all the NCTs, and show the interval classifications of the suspensions.

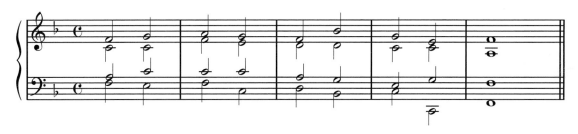

D.   Compose a simple melody for each figured bass below and fill in inner voices to make
     a four-part texture. Include some of the NCTs studied in this chapter. Analyze chords
     and NCTs.

1

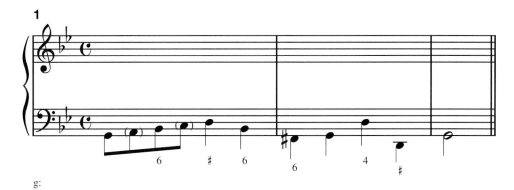

g:

In this example, use a V chord on beat 3 of m. 1. Also, the symbols "6 – –" mean that a first inversion chord is to be maintained throughout m. 2.

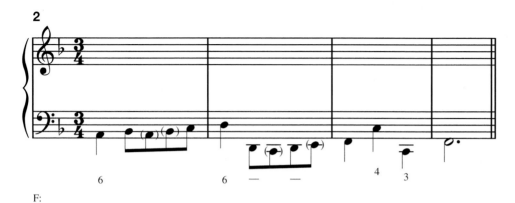

E. Compose a passage in four parts in the key of b minor employing a 7-6 suspension near the beginning and a tonic pedal near the end.

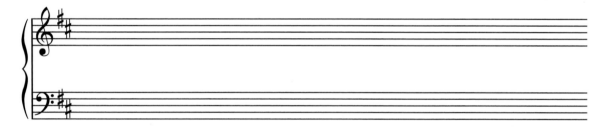

F. Compose eight measures to continue Part A, number 3, on page 72 of this workbook. Maintain a similar texture and end with a PAC. Include an NCT studied in this chapter.

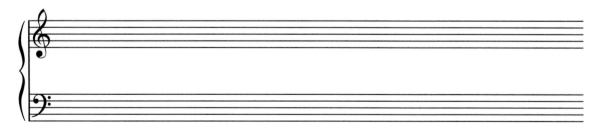

G. The framework below is a simplified version of a passage from Mozart's *Magic Flute.* Embellish the framework, turning it into a vocal part (to be sung on neutral syllables) with piano accompaniment. Try to include at least one chromatic NCT.

H. Continue your solution to Part G to form a parallel period.

Chapter   13

THE V⁷ CHORD

EXERCISE 13-1

A. The note given in each case is the root, 3rd, 5th, or 7th of a V⁷ chord. Notate the chord
    in root position and name the major key in which it would be the V⁷.

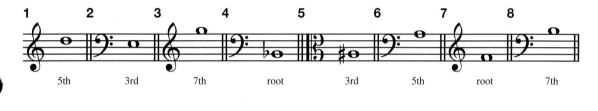

1	2	3	4	5	6	7	8
5th	3rd	7th	root	3rd	5th	root	7th

B. Analyze chords and NCTs in the excerpt below. Then discuss the voice leading in the
    two V⁷ chords. (Note: You might have analyzed the B's in the V chords as passing
    tones, but consider them to be chord 7ths for the purposes of your discussion.)

Bach, "Wir Christenleut' "

C. Resolve each chord to a root position I. (Note: *c* means complete chord, *i* means incomplete chord.)

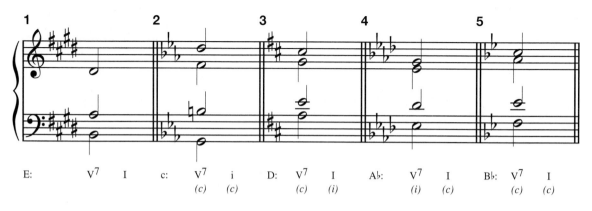

E: V⁷   I   c: V⁷   i   D: V⁷   I   A♭:   V⁷   I   B♭:   V⁷   I
         (c)   *(c)*   *(c)*   *(i)*   *(i)*   *(c)*   *(c)*   *(c)*

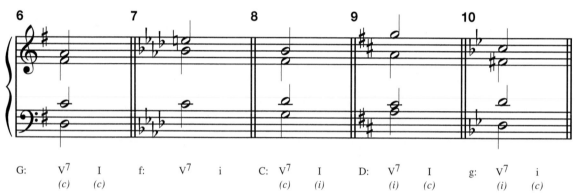

G: V⁷   I   f: V⁷   i   C: V⁷   I   D: V⁷   I   g: V⁷   i
(c)   *(c)*   *(c)*   *(i)*   *(i)*   *(c)*   *(i)*   *(c)*

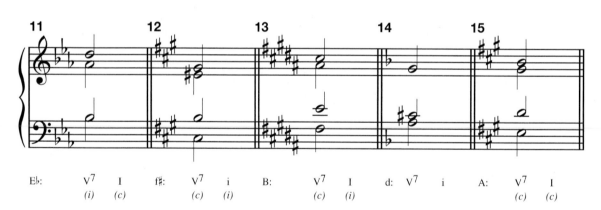

E♭:   V⁷   I   f♯:   V⁷   i   B: V⁷   I   d: V⁷   i   A: V⁷   I
(i)   *(c)*   *(c)*   *(i)*   *(c)*   *(i)*   *(c)*   *(c)*

D.   Notate the key signature and the V^7 chord and then resolve it.

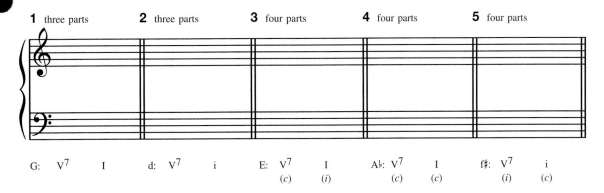

1 three parts	**2** three parts	**3** four parts	**4** four parts	**5** four parts
G: V^7 I	d: V^7 i	E: V^7 I	A♭: V^7 I	f♯: V^7 i
		(c) (i)	(c) (c)	(i) (c)

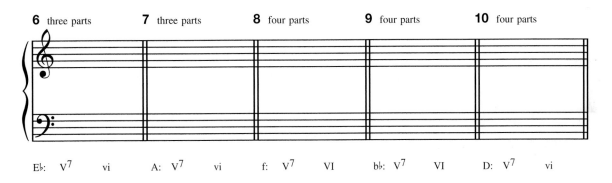

6 three parts	**7** three parts	**8** four parts	**9** four parts	**10** four parts
E♭: V^7 vi	A: V^7 vi	f: V^7 VI	b♭: V^7 VI	D: V^7 vi

E. Analyze the chords specified by this figured bass. Then make two harmonizations, one
    for SAB chorus and one for SATB chorus.

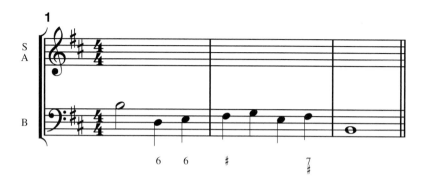

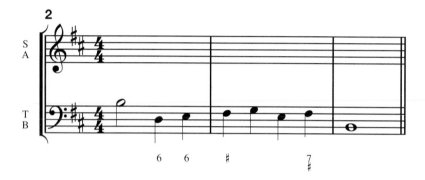

F. Analyze the chords implied by the soprano and bass lines below. Then fill in inner
    parts. Remember that the tenor part sounds a P8 lower than written.

G. Analyze the harmonies implied by these soprano/bass frameworks. Then make four-part versions with embellishments and at least one root position V⁷ chord.

1

2

3

H. Set a short text for four-part chorus. The text might be a poem, a headline from a newspaper, or anything. Include at least one V^7–I progression. Try to keep the motion going through the use of elaborations.

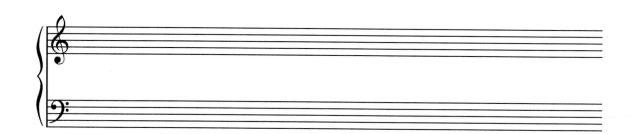

I.   Compose a period in a simple three-part texture. End the first phrase with a V^7–vi DC,
     the second with a V^7–I PAC. Then create a version for three instruments, the top part
     being elaborated by arpeggiations and NCTs, the other two parts in an accompanying
     role. Turn in both versions.

   1. Simple version

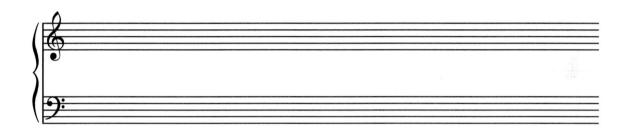

2. Elaborated version

EXERCISE 13-2

A. Notate the specified chords. Use accidentals instead of key signatures.

B. Label chords and NCTs in the excerpts below. Comment on the treatment of the leading tone and 7th in any V^7 chords in root position or inversion.

Notice that in Exercises 1 and 3 the key signature does not agree with the given key. This is because in each case the music has modulated (changed key) to the dominant. Modulation will be introduced in Chapter 18.

1. Bach, "Ich dank' dir, lieber Herre"

(Which is the more sensible analysis of beat 4 of m. 3: iii^6_4 or V^6?)

F:

2. Beethoven, Sonata Op. 2, No. 1, III

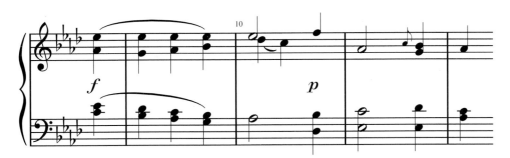

3. Mozart, Quintet K. 452, I (piano reduction)

Bb:

4. Schumann, "Im Westen," Op. 25, No. 23

(Do not label NCTs in this excerpt.)

mich   und mein   Kind - lein   an's   Herz _____ ged - rückt.

C.   Resolve each chord to a tonic triad (except as indicated). Analyze both chords.

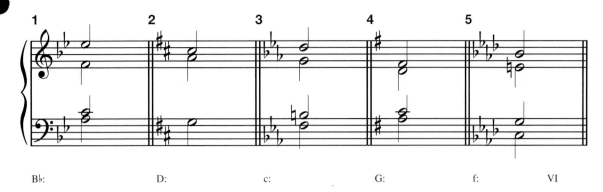

Bb: D: c: G: f: VI

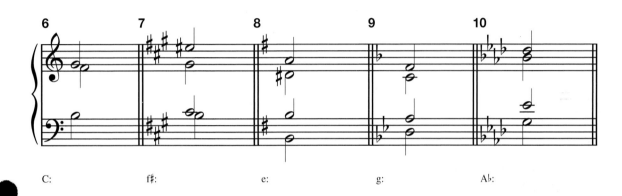

C: f#:   e: g: Ab:

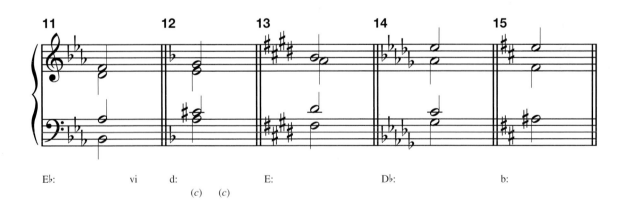

Eb: vi   d: E: Db: b:
                           (c)   (c)

D. Supply the key signature. Then notate and resolve the specified chord. Finally, begin
the passage with a chord that will allow good voice leading and provide the indicated
approach to the 7th. Notate as quarter notes. Label all unlabeled chords.

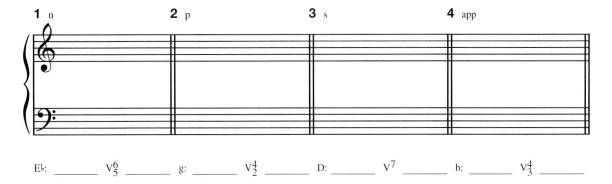

Eb: _____ V$^6_5$ _____   g: _____ V$^4_2$ _____   D: _____ V^7 _____   b: _____ V$^4_3$ _____

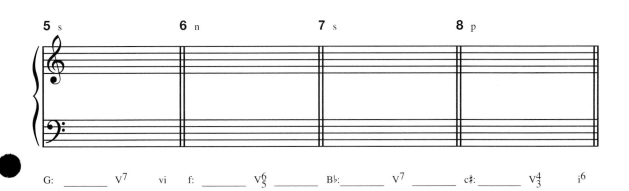

G: _____ V^7 vi   f: _____ V$^6_5$ _____   Bb: _____ V^7 _____   c#: _____ V$^4_3$ i^6

E: _____ V^7 _____   c: _____ V$^4_2$ _____   Ab: _____ V$^4_3$ I   f#: _____ V^7 VI

E. Show with roman numerals the chords that this figured bass calls for. Then complete the realization in four voices.

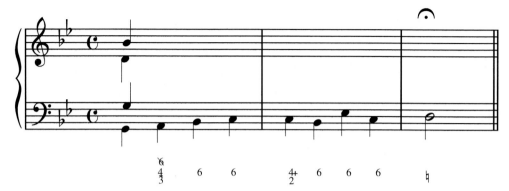

F.   Analyze the chords implied by each soprano/bass framework. Then add inner parts
and embellishments to make a four-part choral texture. Include an inverted V^7 chord.

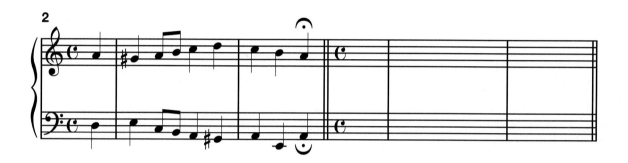

G. Analyze the chords implied by this soprano/bass framework. Then create a piano tex-
    ture by filling out some of the chords and adding embellishments. Arpeggiations will
    be especially useful for prolonging the I chord in mm. 1 to 2. Be sure to include an
    inverted V^7 chord.

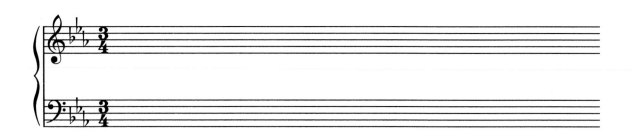

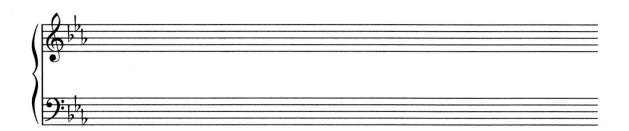

H. Make one or more settings of the following song.

   1. Write an arrangement for two B♭ trumpets, unaccompanied. Analyze the harmonies implied by the two lines. Include at least one inverted V^7.

   2. Make an arrangement for four-part chorus. Try to elaborate the other voices slightly. Include at least one inverted V^7. Watch out for parallel 8ves and 5ths throughout.

   3. Compose a version for piano solo, including at least one inverted V^7. Be prepared to play it or find someone else in the class who will do so.

I.   Compose a period for a string trio (violin, viola, cello) or for some other combination of instruments in your class. Include at least two inverted V^7 chords.

Chapter 14

THE II⁷ AND VII⁷ CHORDS

EXERCISE 14-1

A. Notate the following chords. Use accidentals, not key signatures.

g: vii°⁷   C: ii⁷   e: vii°⁴₂   E♭:   ii⁴₃   D: vii⌀⁶₅   f♯:   ii⌀⁴₃   G: vii⁷   A♭:   ii⁷

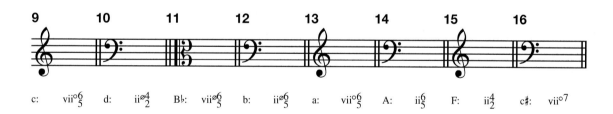

c: vii°⁶₅   d: ii⌀⁴₂   B♭:   vii⌀⁶₅   b: ii⌀⁶₅   a: vii°⁶₅   A: ii⁶₅   F: ii⁴₂   c♯:   vii°⁷

B. Analyze the following chords. Be sure your symbols indicate chord quality and inversion.

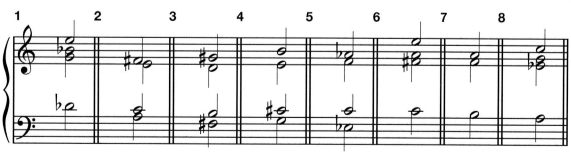

f: ____   G: ____   f♯: ____   D: ____   E♭: ____   e: ____   C: ____   g: ____

C. Analyze the chords and NCTs in the following excerpts. Whenever a ii^7 (ii$^{\varnothing7}$) or vii$^{\varnothing7}$ (vii$^{\circ7}$) chord in root position or inverted is encountered, discuss the voice leading into and out of the chord.

1. Bach, "Jesu, der du meine Seele"

2. Bach, "Herzliebster Jesu, was hast du verbrochen"

b:

3. Bach, *Well-Tempered Clavier,* Book I, Prelude I

C:

4. Label the chords in the blanks provided. Do not label NCTs in this excerpt. The *m.v.* dynamic markings stand for *mezza voce,* "half voice," which means approximately the same thing as *mezzo forte,* or *mf.* The tempo is *Poco Adagio.*

Haydn, Quartet Op. 50, No. 6, II

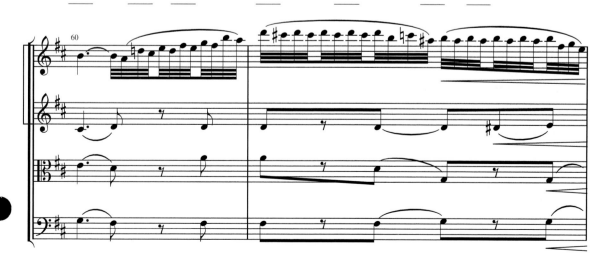

5. Label the chords and NCTs in this excerpt. These are the third and fourth phrases of the double period that makes up the opening theme. Although too long to be quoted here, the entire theme (mm. 1–30) is worth studying.

Haydn, Quartet Op. 20, No. 4, I

D. Notate, introduce, and resolve the specified chords. Approach each chord 7th as a suspension, a neighbor, or a passing tone, as specified. Include key signatures and roman numerals.

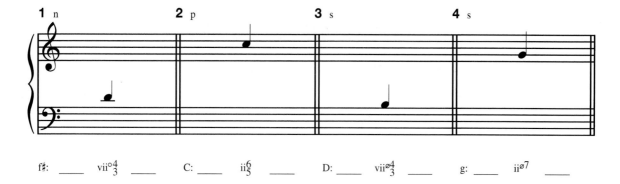

f♯: ____ vii°$^4_3$ ____   C: ____ ii$^6_5$ ____   D: ____ vii°$^4_3$ ____   g: ____ ii^{ø7} ____

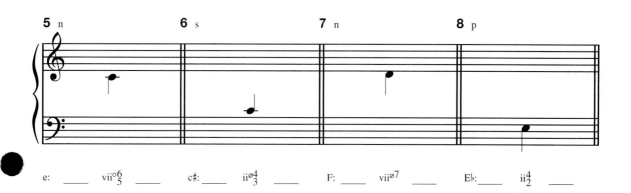

e: ____ vii°$^6_5$ ____   c♯: ____ ii$^{ø4}_3$ ____   F: ____ vii^{ø7} ____   E♭: ____ ii$^4_2$ ____

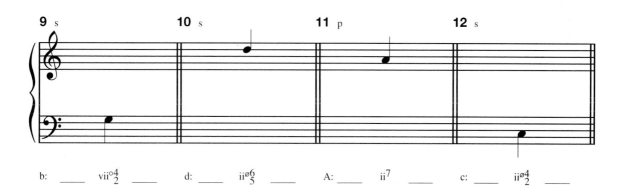

b: ____ vii°$^4_2$ ____   d: ____ ii$^{ø6}_5$ ____   A: ____ ii^7 ____   c: ____ ii$^{ø4}_2$ ____

E. Analyze these figured basses and continue the realizations, keeping the keyboard texture but following conventional partwriting procedures.

1.

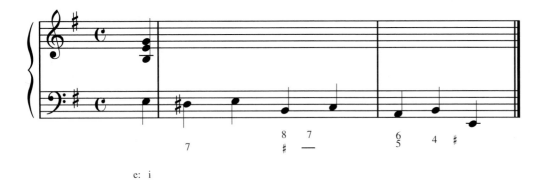

e: i

2. Bach, St. Matthew Passion, No. 20

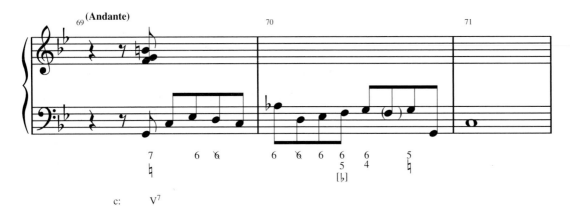

c: V⁷

F. Harmonize these chorale phrases for four-part chorus.

1. Include a root position ii^7.

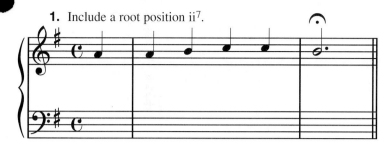

G:

2. Include a root position vii$^{\circ7}$ and a 4-3 suspension.

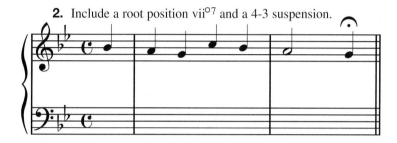

g:

3. Include a ii$^{\varnothing 4}_{2}$ and a deceptive cadence. Some eighth-note chords will be necessary.

d:

4. Include a vii$^{\varnothing 4}_{3}$ and a passing tone.

C:

G. Make a setting of the folk song below for some combination of voices and/or instruments available in your class. Include one of the chords discussed in this chapter.

Chapter 15

OTHER DIATONIC SEVENTH CHORDS

EXERCISE 15-1

A. Notate the following chords. Use accidentals, not key signatures.

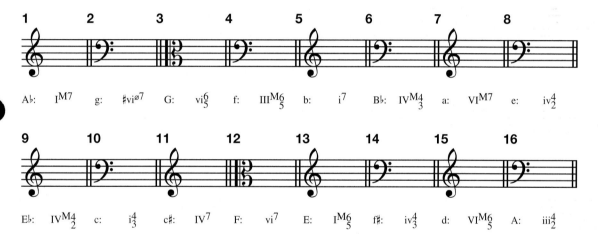

Ab: I^{M7} g: #vi^{ø7} G: vi$^6_5$ f: III$^{M6}_5$ b: i^7 Bb: IV$^{M4}_3$ a: VI^{M7} e: iv$^4_2$

Eb: IV$^{M4}_2$ c: i$^4_3$ c#: IV^7 F: vi^7 E: I$^{M6}_5$ f#: iv$^4_3$ d: VI$^{M6}_5$ A: iii$^4_2$

B. Analyze the following chords. Be sure your symbols indicate chord quality and inversion.

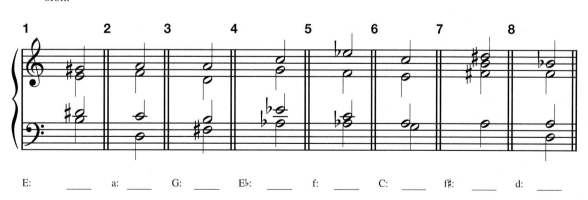

E: ____   a: ____   G: ____   Eb: ____   f: ____   C: ____   f#: ____   d: ____

C. Analyze the chords in the excerpts below. Comment on the voice leading involving any of the chords discussed in this chapter.

1. Chopin, Mazurka in a minor, Op. Posth.

2. Bach, "Herr Jesu Christ, du höchstes Gut"

3. Corelli, Concerto Grosso Op. 6, No. 1, VII

D: iii

4. Haydn, Piano Sonata No. 30, I

After you finish labeling all of the chords, complete the three-part reduction of mm. 86–92 that follows the excerpt. The neighbor figures in 16th notes in mm. 84–91 are NCTs, not the sevenths of chords.

f#:

Textural reduction

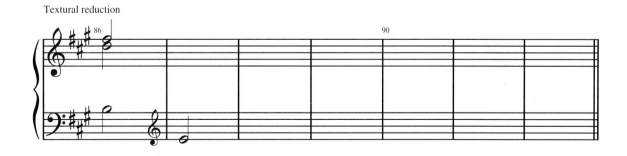

D. Continue this four-part elaboration of Example 15-19 (p. 238).

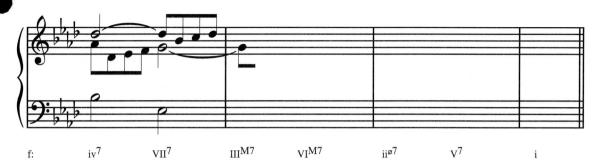

f: iv⁷   VII⁷   III^{M7} VI^{M7} ii^{ø7} V⁷   i

E. Notate, introduce, and resolve the specified chords. Approach each chord 7th as a suspension, a neighbor, or a passing tone, as specified. Include key signatures and roman numerals.

1 p   **2** s   **3** p   **4** s

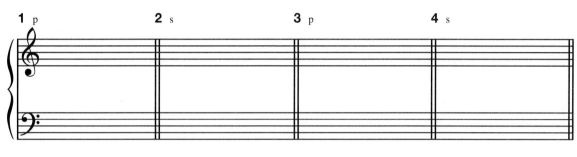

F: ___ iii⁷ ___   E: ___ IV$^{M6}_5$ ___   g: ___ i$^6_5$ ___   b: ___ ♯vi^{ø7} ___

5 n   **6** s   **7** p   **8** s

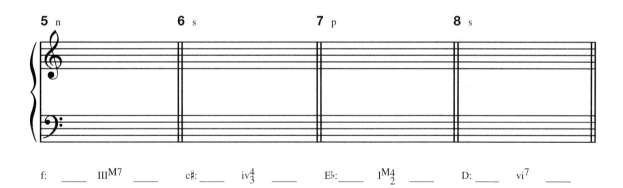

f: ___ III^{M7} ___   c♯: ___ iv$^4_3$ ___   E♭: ___ I$^{M4}_2$ ___   D: ___ vi⁷ ___

9 s   **10** s   **11** s   **12** n

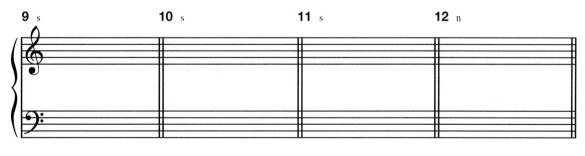

G: ___ $^6_5$ IV$^{M4}_2$ ___ $^6_5$ c: ___ ⁷ VI$^{M4}_3$ ___ ⁷   B♭: ___ ⁷ I^{M7} ___ ⁷   d: ___ IV$^6_5$ ___

(circle of fifths)   (circle of fifths)   (circle of fifths)

F.   Analyze the chords called for by the figured bass below. Remember that the figured bass symbols are part of the music, not part of the harmonic analysis, which should be written beneath it. Then continue the four-part realization of that figured bass. Note: Be sure to review pages 176–177 before proceeding. (Figures in the fifth measure added by the authors.)

Corelli, Concerto Grosso Op. 6, No. 12, V

G. Analyze this figured bass and continue the realization, keeping the keyboard texture but following conventional partwriting procedures.

Corelli, Concerto Gross, Op. 6 No. 9, "Preludio"

H. Compose a passage for three voices or instruments containing a sequence of seventh chords similar to that used in the excerpt of Part F.

I. The following is a simple note-against-note contrapuntal framework. Analyze the implied harmonies, then elaborate it into a passage containing several seventh chords. Use four parts or a free keyboard texture. Your final version might be complex, but the original framework should be retained. Include roman numerals and NCT analysis.

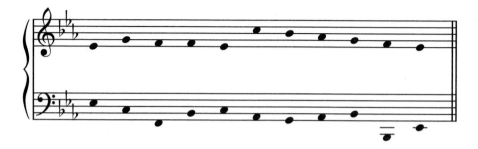

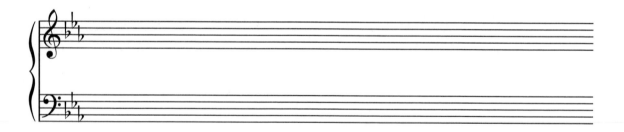

J.   Create a framework similar to Exercise I but in the minor mode. Be sure that it implies a good harmonic progression. Then create an elaboration that employs some of the seventh chords discussed in this chapter. If possible, score for a combination of instruments in your class.

Chapter   16

SECONDARY FUNCTIONS 1

EXERCISE 16-1

A. Review the material on spelling secondary dominants (p. 248). Then notate these secondary dominants in the specified inversions. Include key signatures.

1	2	3	4	5
c♯: V^7/iv	A♭: V^6/V	c: V^4_3/VI	e: V^6/III	F: V^4_2/ii

6	7	8	9	10
D: V^6/vi	b: V^7/V	A: V^6_5/iii	g: V/iv	a: V^4_2/V

11	12	13	14	15
E♭: V^6_5/IV	f♯: V^6/VII	C: V^7/ii	B♭: V^4_2/IV	G: V^4_3/V

B. Label any chord that might be a secondary dominant according to the steps outlined
    on page 248–249. Label all others with an *x*.

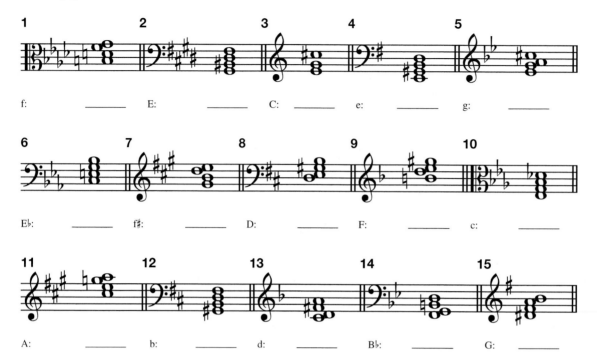

f: _____   E: _____   C: _____   e: _____   g: _____

Eb: _____   f#: _____   D: _____   F: _____   c: _____

A: _____   b: _____   d: _____   Bb: _____   G: _____

EXERCISE 16-2

A. Analysis.

1. Label chords and NCTs. Identify any six-four chords by type. This excerpt contains a set of parallel 5ths in a context that Bach must have found acceptable because he used them so often in this situation. See if you can find them.

Bach, "Freuet euch, ihr Christen alle"

f:

2. Label chords and NCTs. Notice that the right hand is in bass clef throughout. Discuss the sequence implied by mm. 5 to 8. Is the excerpt an example of a period? If so, is it a parallel period or a contrasting period?

Beethoven, Sonata Op. 13, II

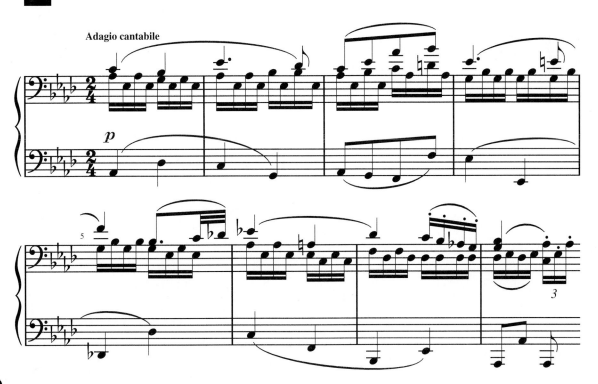

3. Label the chords with roman numerals. Thinking in terms of chord roots, find
the longest harmonic sequence in this excerpt.

Beethoven, Sonata Op. 2, No. 1, I

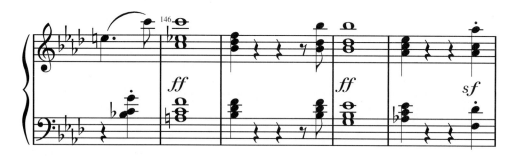

4. Label chords and NCTs. Ignore the grace notes in your harmonic and NCT analysis; for example, the E♭5 in m. 1 is an upper neighbor ornamented by the appoggiatura grace note. Comment on Chopin's use of F♯ and F♮ in this excerpt. Where do they occur? Are they ever in conflict? The form of the excerpt is a (parallel/contrasting) (period/double period).

Chopin, Mazurka Op. 67, No. 2

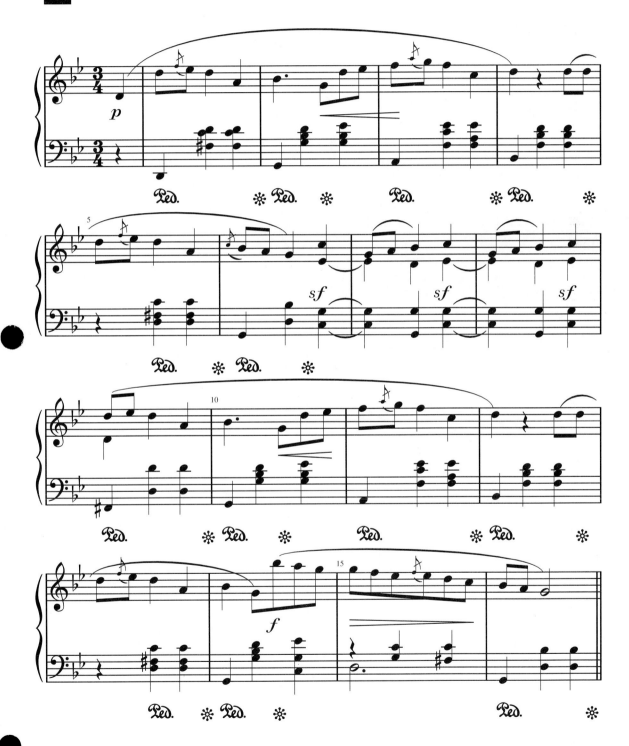

5. Label chords and NCTs. What is the form of this excerpt? (Note: Measures 1–2 are introductory.)

Beethoven, Quartet Op. 135, III

6. Label the chords with roman numerals. Label NCTs in the solo bassoon part only. The
note under the fermata in m. 49 represents a V chord. It was at this point that the soloist
improvised a cadenza. The conductor waited until he heard the soloist arrive at the G3
(often trilled), at which point he would signal the orchestra to be ready for their entrance
in m. 50.

Mozart, Bassoon Concerto K. 191, II

B. For each of the following problems, first analyze the given chord. Next, find a smooth way to lead into the chord. Although there are many possibilities, it will often work to use a chord whose root is a P5 above the root of the secondary dominant. Experiment with other relationships also. Then resolve each chord properly, taking special care with the leading tone and 7th resolutions. Analyze all chords.

g: ____ ____ ____   C: ____ ____   G: ____ ____ V^6_5/V E: ____ ____ ____   A♭: ____ ____

D: ____ ____ ____   B♭: ____ ____ ii^7 f: ____ ____ ____   c: ____ ____ ____   a: ____ ____ ____

C. List below each note the secondary V and V⁷ chords that could harmonize that note. You might find it helpful to refer to the charts on page 247.

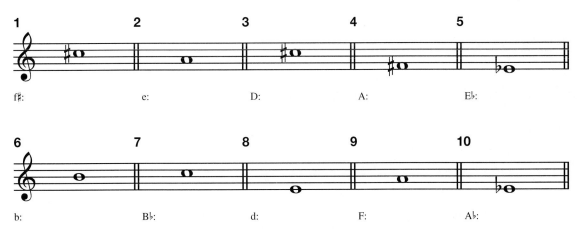

f♯:   e: D: A: E♭:

b: B♭:   d: F: A♭:

D. Provide roman numerals to show how the first note could be harmonized as a second-
    ary dominant. The second note should be harmonized by the tonicized chord.

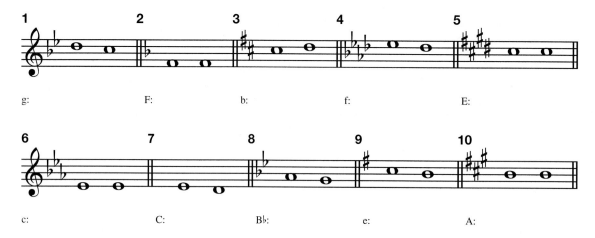

g: F: b: f: E:

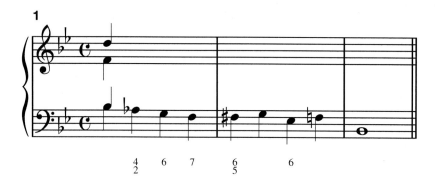

c: C: B♭:   e: A:

E. Analyze the chords specified by each figured bass, then make an arrangement for
    SATB chorus. Strive for smooth voice leading, even if this results in a dull soprano
    line.

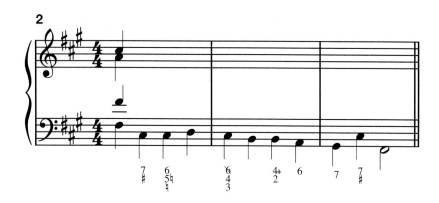

F. Harmonize each chorale phrase for SATB chorus. Include one or more secondary
    dominants in each phrase and activate the texture with some NCTs.

Eb: d:

C:

g:

G. Analyze the harmonies implied by the following soprano/bass framework. Then make
    a more interesting version for piano, beginning with the two measures given below.

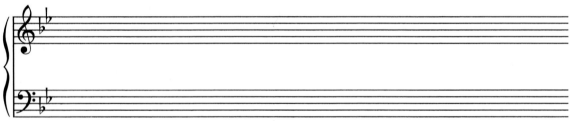

H. Continue the example below to make a total of at least eight measures. Include one or more secondary dominants and end with a PAC. Then score it for four instruments found in your class. Analyze all chords and NCTs.

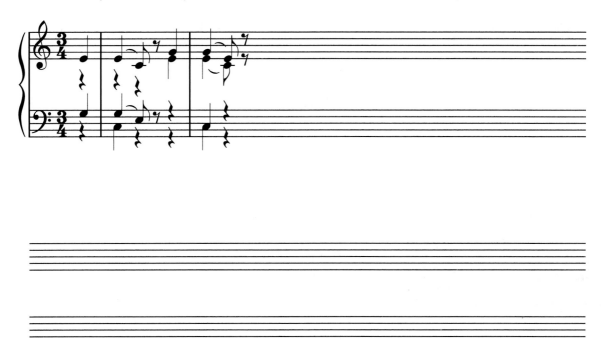

I.   Finish the analysis of the phrase below. This phrase is to serve as the *a* phrase of a
     longer theme you will compose. The theme will be in the form of a parallel double
     period. Include at least one secondary dominant.

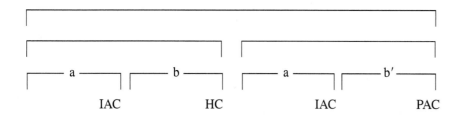

A: (I) (V⁷)   I

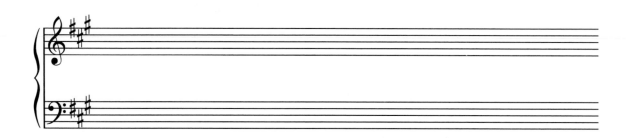

Chapter 17

SECONDARY FUNCTIONS 2

EXERCISE 17-1

A. Review how to spell secondary leading-tone chords (pp. 264–265). Then notate these secondary leading-tone chords in the specified inversion. Include key signatures.

1	2	3	4	5
A: vii°⁶/iii	F: vii°⁶/ii	c: vii°⁶/VI	E: vii°⁶₅/IV	A♭: vii°⁷/IV

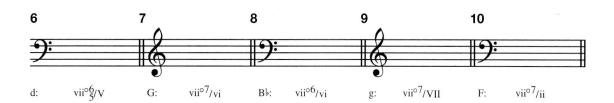

6	7	8	9	10
d: vii°⁶₅/V	G: vii°⁷/vi	B♭: vii°⁶/vi	g: vii°⁷/VII	F: vii°⁷/ii

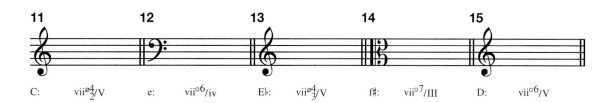

11	12	13	14	15
C: vii°⁴₂/V	e: vii°⁶/iv	E♭: viiø⁴₃/V	f♯: vii°⁷/III	D: vii°⁶/V

B. Label any chord that would be a secondary leading-tone chord according to the steps
    outlined on page 265. Label all others with an *x*.

c: _____   G: _____   A: _____   B♭: _____   e: _____

C: _____   d: _____   E: _____   E♭: _____   A♭: _____

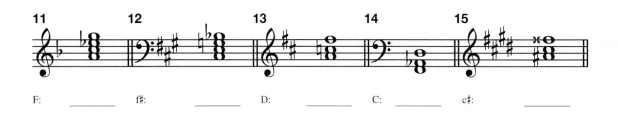

F: _____   f♯: _____   D: _____   C: _____   c♯: _____

EXERCISE 17-2

A. Analysis.

   1. In the brilliant and witty concluding passage below, Mozart combines the antecedent
   and consequent phrases from the beginning of the minuet (marked *a* and *b* in mm.
   55–58).

   a. Mark all occurrences of *a* and *b*.

   b. Find where the *b* phrase is used in imitation.

   c. Find inverted (upside down) statements of *a* and *b*.

   d. Find a place where original and inverted statements of *b* occur simultaneously.

   e. Put roman numerals in the blanks provided. NCTs are in parentheses.

   Mozart, String Quartet K. 464, II

2. Label the chords with roman numerals (the Italian augmented sixth chord in m. 4 will be discussed in Chapter 23). Use your imagination and your ear in analyzing the last chord in m. 2.

Schumann, "Die Löwenbraut," Op. 31, No. 1

3. Label chords and NCTs. (An optional piano accompaniment is omitted from the example.) What is the form of this excerpt?

Brahms, "Und gehst du über den Kirchhof," Op. 44

4. Analyze chords and NCTs. Find two circle-of-fifths progressions that contain more than four chords. What is the form of this excerpt?

Tchaikovsky, "Morning Prayer," Op. 39, No. 1

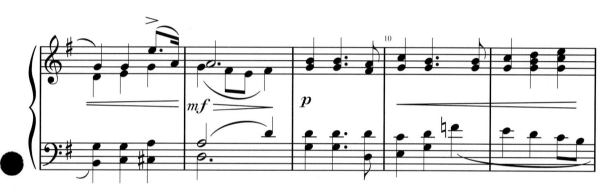

5. This short song is given here in its entirety. Analyze the chords and NCTs. There are some places where alternative analyses are possible—in m. 1, for example, where the line G♯–F♯–E could be analyzed as chord tones or as passing tones. Think of two analyses for the second chord in m. 11, one of them being a secondary function.

Schumann, "Aus meinen Thränen spriessen," Op. 48, No. 2

B. For each of these problems, first analyze and resolve the given chord, being especially careful with the chord 7th and the leading tone. Then find a smooth way to lead into the given chord. Analyze all chords.

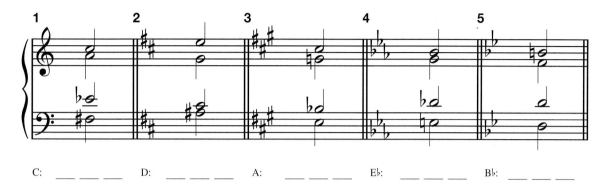

C: ___ ___ ___   D: ___ ___ ___   A: ___ ___ ___   E♭: ___ ___ ___   B♭: ___ ___ ___

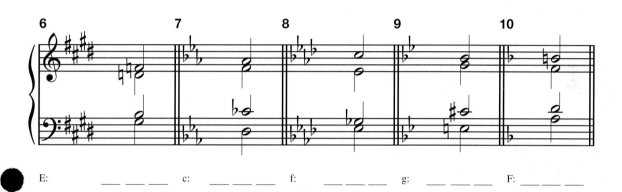

E: ___ ___ ___   c: ___ ___ ___   f: ___ ___ ___   g: ___ ___ ___   F: ___ ___ ___

C. Analyze the harmonies specified by each figured bass and make an arrangement for SATB chorus. Try to use smooth voice leading, even at the expense of an interesting soprano line.

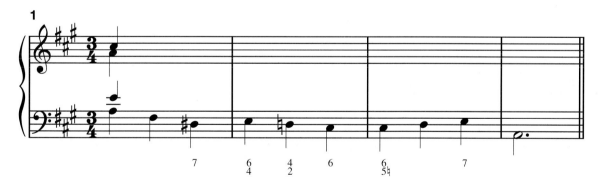

2

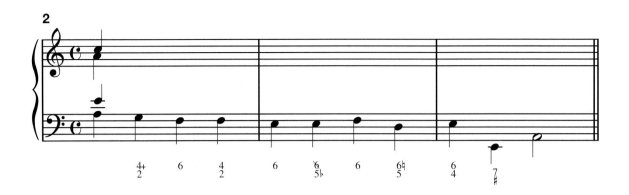

D. Harmonize each of these chorale phrases for SATB chorus. Include at least one sec-
    ondary leading-tone chord or incorporate some other aspect discussed in this chapter
    in each harmonization.

1

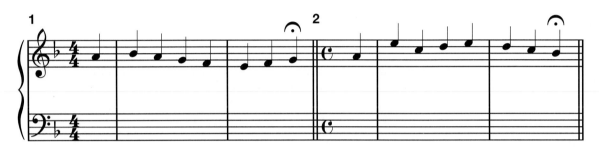

F:

a:

3

F:

E. Each item below contains two versions of the same excerpt, one of them in a simple texture and one more elaborate. Continue the simple texture first, including some aspect of harmony discussed in this chapter. Then continue the elaboration, using your simple version as a framework. Label chords and NCTs.

1a.

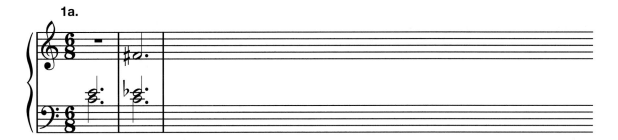

1b.

Andantino

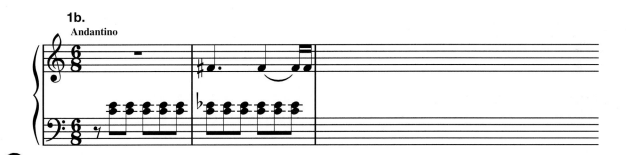

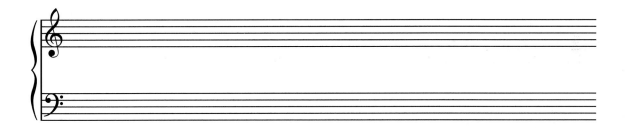

2a.

2b.

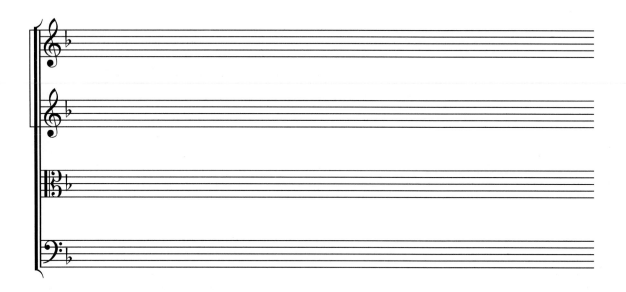

F. Compose a setting of the following poem for chorus (three, four, or five parts) or for solo voice with piano accompaniment. Use at least one secondary leading-tone chord and one deceptive resolution of a secondary dominant. Try to put your special harmonic effects at appropriate places in the text. (Use either or both stanzas.)

A bird came down the walk;
He did not know I saw;
He bit an angle-worm in halves
And ate the fellow raw.

And then he drank a dew
From a convenient grass,
And then hopped sidewise to the wall
To let a beetle pass.

—From "A bird came down the walk" by Emily Dickinson

Chapter 18

MODULATIONS USING DIATONIC COMMON CHORDS

EXERCISE 18-1

A.   Name the relative key in each case.

1. Gb _____   **6.** d _____

2. A _____   **7.** F♯ _____

3. e _____   **8.** c♯ _____

4. g _____   **9.** Ab _____

5. C♯ _____   **10.** ab _____

B.   Name all the keys closely related to the given key. Be sure to use uppercase for major, lowercase for minor.

1. b   _____   _____   _____   _____   _____

2. eb _____   _____   _____   _____   _____

3. G   _____   _____   _____   _____   _____

4. B   _____   _____   _____   _____   _____

5. F   _____   _____   _____   _____   _____

6. f♯ _____   _____   _____   _____   _____

C.   Name the relationship in each case (enharmonically equivalent, parallel, relative and closely related, closely related, foreign).

1. D/e _____   **6.** Ab/Cb _____

2. eb/Gb _____   **7.** C♯/Db _____

3. A/a _____   **8.** g♯/c♯ _____

4. d♯/G _____   **9.** ab/bb _____

5. Bb/F _____   **10.** c/Eb _____

EXERCISE 18-2

A. Analysis.

   1. This excerpt modulates from B♭ to F, its dominant. Label the chords, being sure to show two roman numerals for the common chord. The blanks beneath the music show where the bass changes, but not where the common chord occurs. NCTs in mm. 1 and 8 (only) have been identified for you.

Szymanowska, Nocturne

   2. Label chords and NCTs in this chorale, which is presented in its entirety. Which two phrases are very similar melodically? What portion of these phrases is harmonized similarly? What chord is emphasized in the first half of the second of these two phrases?

Bach, "Uns ist ein Kindlein heut' geborn"

3. This example, also a complete chorale, is in g minor, although it ends with a major triad (the "Picardy third"). Label chords, but not the NCTs. Notice how often the melody follows an arch contour (inverted in the second phrase). Bracket those arch contours in the melody. If you find any similar contours in the bass, bracket them also.

Bach, "Jesu, der du meine Seele"

4. Label the chords with roman numerals. How do the pickup notes at the beginning of the excerpt help smooth the return to the first key when the repeat is taken?

Mozart, Sonata K. 330, II

5. Label the chords with roman numerals.

Fanny Mendelssohn Hensel, "Das Meer erglänzte weit hinaus."

6. Listen to this song all the way through. Then list every tonality that is touched on in the song, either by simple tonicization or by modulation. Which (other than tonic) is referred to again at the end of the song? Decide on one or two tonalities (other than tonic) that represent modulations rather than tonicizations. Then label all chords with roman numerals.

Schumann, "Wenn ich in deine Augen seh'," Op. 48, No. 4

7. This excerpt begins in A♭ and ends in g minor, modulating through yet another key in the process. Label all chords, and label the NCTs in the vocal part. The German augmented sixth chord in m. 49 will be discussed in a later chapter.

Mozart, Marriage of Figaro, K. 492, "Voi che sapete"

8. Label the chords with roman numerals. In an Alberti bass accompaniment, such as the left hand in this example, the bass note for each chord is usually considered to be the lowest note struck. So in m. 9 the only *bass* notes are D and C♯.

Beethoven, Sonata Op. 10, No. 3, II

B. Fill in the name of the new key on the second line of each exercise.

1. e: i $\text{ii}°^6$ V^4_2 | i^6 iv^6 |

     ____: i^6 V^4_2 i^6 $\text{ii}°^6$ V^7 i

2. D: I   V | I^6 $\text{vii}°^6$ |

     ____: $\text{ii}°^6$ i^6_4 V   i   (V)

3. F: I $\text{vii}°^6$ | I^6 vi |

     ____: ii $\text{vii}°^6$ I V^6_5 I

4. g: i V^6_5 V^4_2/iv $\text{iv}6$ | V i^6 |

     ____: iv^6 $\text{ii}°^6$ V^7 i

5. b: i $\text{ii}ø^4_2$ V^6_5 i   VI iv^6 |

     ____: ii^6 I^6_4 V^7 I   (V)

6. E♭:   I ii^6 | V   vi |

     ____: iv $\text{ii}ø^6_5$ V   VI   iv   V   i

7. A: I V^4_3 | I^6 V^6 |

     ____: IV^6 V^6_5 i $\text{ii}ø^6_5$ i^6_4 V^7 i   (V)

8. c: i V^7 | VI   iv |

     ____: vi IV^6 (I^6_4) ii^6_5 V   I

C. List the diatonic triads that could serve as common chords between each pair of keys.
    In minor keys, assume the usual chord qualities: i, ii°, III, iv, V, VI, vii°.

ex.	First key, C:	I	iii	V	vi
	Triads:	C	e	G	a
	Second key, G:	IV	vi	I	ii

1. First key, E:
   Triads:
   Second key, f♯:

2. First key, D♭:
   Triads:
   Second key, G♭:

3. First key, c:
   Triads:
   Second key, B♭:

4. First key, f:
   Triads:
   Second key, A♭:

5. First key, B:
   Triads:
   Second key, F♯:

6. First key, A♭:
   Triads:
   Second key, B♭:

D. Choose two of the progressions from Part B. Arrange one for SATB chorus and the
    other for SAB chorus. Activate the texture with NCTs and/or arpeggiations. Arrange
    the metric and rhythmic structure so that the last chord comes on a strong beat. Label
    chords and NCTs.

E.   Harmonize the following chorale tunes for SATB chorus.

   1.   In the first phrase, modulate from i to III. The second phrase should return to i.

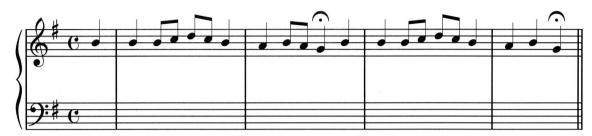

   2.   Modulate from I to vi in phrase 1. Return to I in phrase 2.

F.   Analyze the chords specified by this figured bass and then make an arrangement for SATB chorus.

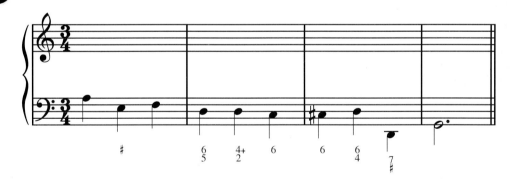

G. Continue this soprano/bass framework, analyzing the implied harmonies. Phrase 1 (mm. 1–4) should end with a HC in f. Phrase 2 (mm. 5–8) should end with a PAC in A♭. The resulting form is a modulating period. Then arrange for some combination of instruments in your class, filling in as many inner parts as needed. Elaborate your final version with NCTs and arpeggiations.

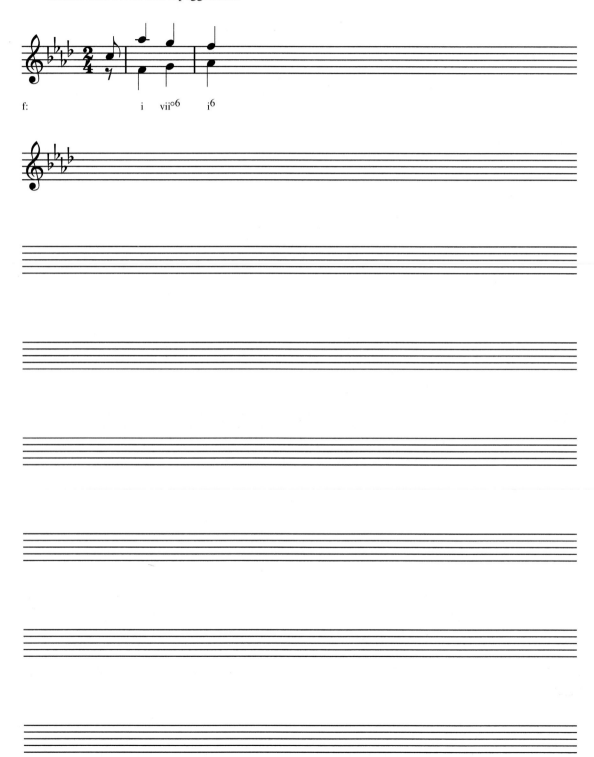

f: i   vii°6   i6

H. Compose a double period for some solo instrument with piano accompaniment. As the diagram indicates, the first phrase stays in A, whereas the second tonicizes (or modulates to) E. Phrase 3 returns briefly to A but turns quickly to D. The fourth phrase returns to A for the final cadence.

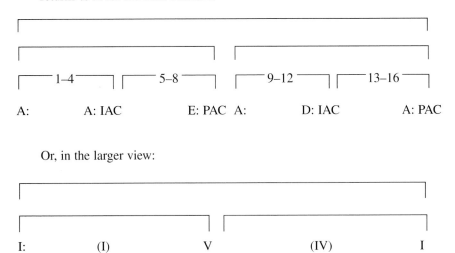

Or, in the larger view:

The beginning of phrase 1 is given below. Compose the soprano/bass framework first.

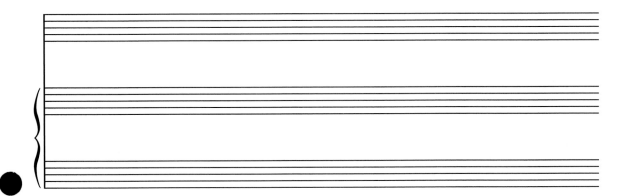

I. Using a text of your own choosing, compose a passage for chorus (three or four parts). If in major, it should have a tonal scheme of I–vi–I–ii–I. If in minor, use i–VI–i–iv–i.

Chapter 19

SOME OTHER
MODULATORY TECHNIQUES

EXERCISE 19-1

A.   Analysis. (Note: Some of the modulations below might be of the diatonic common-chord type.)

    1. a. What three keys are implied in this excerpt?

        b. How would you explain the modulations?

        c. Continue the two-voice reduction below the score but avoid the change of register in m. 36.

        ♫ Beethoven, Sonata Op. 10, No. 1, I

Textural reduction

2. There are two modulations in this excerpt. Label chords and NCTs. At what point does Bach not follow the conventions of spacing discussed on pages 60–61? What is achieved by the spacing he uses? Where is there a sonority used in an unusual bass position? How is the reason for this bass position related to the question about the spacing?

Bach, "Warum betrübst du dich"

3. What two keys are found in this excerpt? How are they related? What is the best way to describe the modulation? Label the chords with roman numerals.

Hüllmandel, *"Un Poco Adagio"*

4. Two distantly related keys are found in this passage. Label chords and NCTs.

Schubert, "Auf dem Flusse," Op. 89, No. 7

Mit har - ter, star - rer Rin - de hast du dich ü - ber - deckt, liegst

kalt und un - be - weg - lich im San - de ___ aus - ge - streckt.

5. This excerpt modulates from F major to what other key? Of excerpts 1 through 4, which
    modulation most closely resembles this one? In what ways? (The chords in mm. 35–36
    are labeled for you because some of them involve concepts discussed in later chapters.)

Mozart, Marriage of Figaro, K. 492, "Voi che sapete"

B. Analyze the harmonies implied by this soprano/bass framework. Add an alto part to
    create a three-part texture. Embellish the texture with a few NCTs, including a 4-3
    suspension. Identify the modulatory technique used.

C. Analyze the implied harmonies and then add alto and tenor parts. Enliven the texture
    with NCTs and/or arpeggiations. Identify the modulatory technique used.

D. Use the framework below as the basis for a repeated period. The second phrase should begin and end in D major (phrase modulation). Compose a first ending that modulates back to F using some modulatory technique discussed in this chapter. Include NCTs and arpeggiations in your final version. Score for piano or some combination of instruments found in your class.

E. The framework below is also to be used as the basis for a repeated period for piano
    (or other instruments). The first phrase is in E♭, and the second should be a sequen-
    tial repetition of the first, in A♭. Write out the repeat of phrases 1 to 2. Use more
    embellishments in the repeat than you used in the first eight measures.

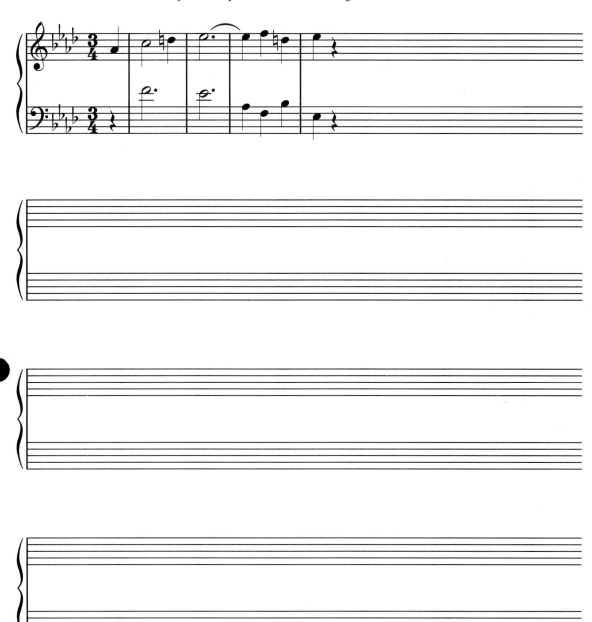

Chapter 20

BINARY AND TERNARY FORMS

EXERCISE 20-1

A. Diagram this excerpt down to the phrase level and name the form. Assume all phrases are four measures long. Also, answer the following questions:

1. What is the form of mm. 1–8?

2. Find and label a vii$^{\circ 4}_{3}$/V and a vii$^{\circ 4}_{3}$/vi.

3. Why do you think Mozart chose to use a double stop in the violas in m. 14? (A double stop is a technique that allows a stringed instrument to play two notes at once.)

Mozart, *Eine kleine Nachtmusik,* III

B. Name the form of this piece (do not diagram phrases and cadences). Watch out for written-out repeats. Also, do or answer the following:

1. Label the chords in mm. 5 to 8.

2. What chord forms the basis of mm. 33 to 39?

3. Analyze the last chord in m. 34.

4. In what measures does the "boom-chick-chick" accompaniment drop out?

Chopin, Mazurka Op. 67, No. 3

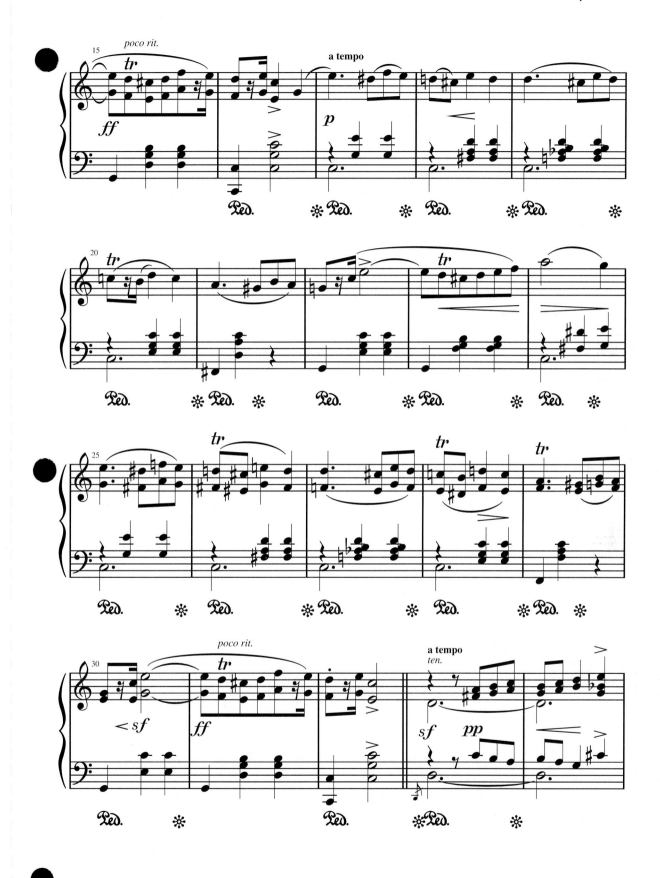

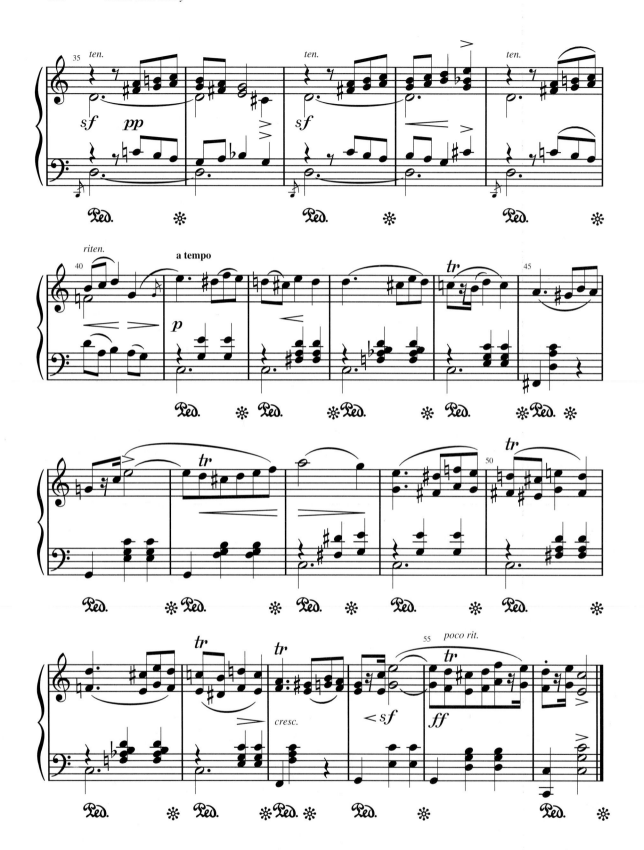

C. This excerpt is the first part of a scherzo and trio (a scherzo is much like a minuet, only faster). The trio is not shown.

   1. Diagram this scherzo at the phrase level. The key implied by mm. 17 to 20 is d minor, not A major.

   2. Identify the form. Do not be misled by the written-out repeat in mm. 9 to 16—this is a two-reprise form.

   3. Find two examples of chromatic mediant relationships.

   Beethoven, Violin Sonata Op. 24, III

D. Diagram this piece down to the phrase level and name the form. Also, answer the following questions:

1. Where is a sequence involving both hands? Bracket it.

2. What does the G♯4 in m. 6 accomplish?

3. What material in mm. 10 to 22 is obviously derived from mm. 1 to 9.

♪ March from the *Notebook for Anna Magdalena Bach*

E. This excerpt, the final movement of a piano sonata, is a minuet and trio, although Haydn did not label it as such.

   1. Diagram phrases and cadences, treating the minuet and trio as separate pieces. Be sure to play or listen to the music because some of the returns are disguised. (A melodically varied return of phrase *a* is still labeled phrase *a*, not phrase *a'*.)

   2. Name the forms of the minuet and the trio.

   3. In performance, the trio is followed by a return to the minuet (although the repeats are omitted), ending at the fermata. What is the form of the movement as a whole?

   4. Find the one phrase in this movement that is not four measures long and compare it to its earlier four-measure version. How does Haydn extend this phrase?

   5. Provide roman numerals for the following chords:

   a. _____ m. 17, beats 1 to 2 (in E♭)

   b. _____ m. 19, beat 3 (in E♭)

   c. _____ m. 35, beat 3 (in A♭)

   d. _____ m. 44 (in A♭)

   e. _____ m. 46, beat 3 (in A♭)

Haydn, Piano Sonata No. 38, III

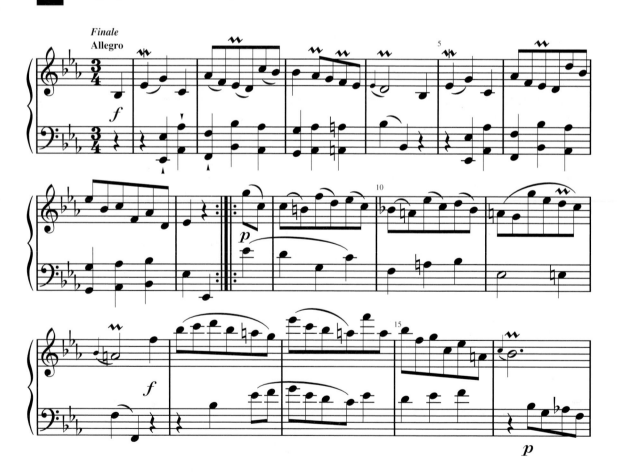

MODE MIXTURE

EXERCISE 21-1

A. Notate these chords in the specified inversions. Include key signatures.

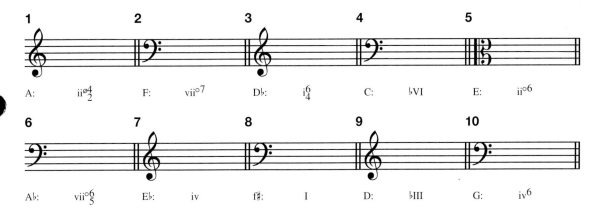

A: ii⌀$^4_2$ F: vii°⁷   D♭: i$^6_4$ C: ♭VI   E: ii°⁶

A♭: vii°$^6_5$ E♭: iv   f♯: I   D: ♭III   G: iv⁶

B. Label these chords. Include inversion symbols.

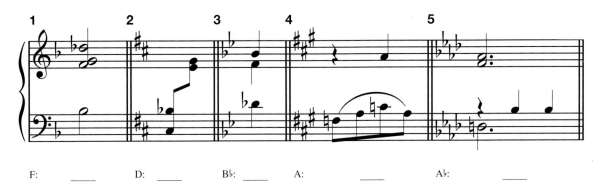

F: _____   D: _____   B♭: _____   A: _____   A♭: _____

G: ____   C: ____   E: ____   d: ____   Eb: ____

C. Analysis.

1. Label the chords with roman numerals. NCTs have been put in parentheses (other interpretations are possible). Which chord could be considered an example of secondary mode mixture?

♪ Bach, "Herr Jesu Christ, wahr'r Mensch und Gott"

C:

2. Label the chords and NCTs. Circle the roman numerals of any borrowed chords.

♪ Schumann, "Ich grolle nicht," Op. 48, No. 7

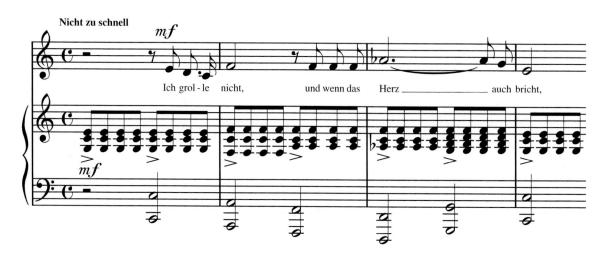

3. Label the chords, circling the roman numerals of any borrowed chords. Label the cadence type.

Brahms, Symphony No. 3, Op. 90, II

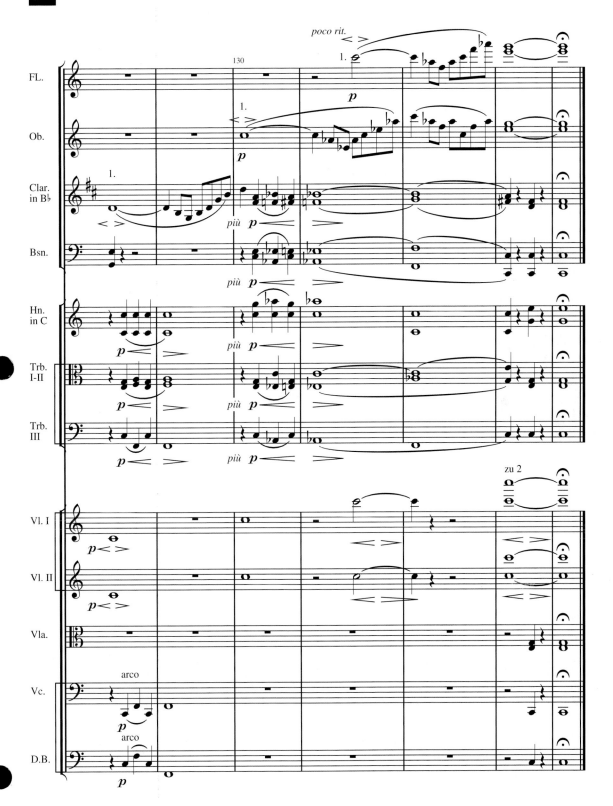

4. Schumann uses mode mixture in this passage to modulate from E to its minor dominant. Label all the chords and the common-chord modulation.

Schumann, "Liebeslied," Op. 51, No. 5

5. In the passage below, Mozart uses mode mixture twice to move from E major to the
very distant key of c minor and then uses mode mixture twice more to return to E major.
Label all chords, including the common-chord modulations from E to c and back.
(Remember that the bass voice is always the lowest-sounding voice, so that the bass
note in m. 221, for example, is the cello G, not the piano E♭.)

Mozart, Piano Trio K. 542, I

6. This excerpt modulates from A♭ to some other key and then back to A♭. Label all chords and NCTs.

Schubert, Impromptu Op. 90, No. 1

D. Part writing. Analyze the chords implied by the soprano/bass framework. Then fill in
    alto and tenor parts. Be sure to use the specified mode mixture.

   1. Include a ii$^{\circ 6}_{5}$.

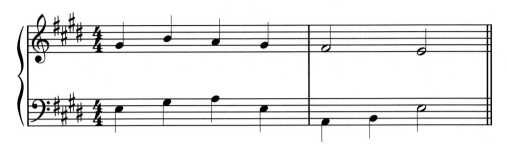

   2. Include a iv^6 and a ii$^{\varnothing 4}_{3}$.

E. The first two phrases of a chorale melody are given below. A bass line is included for
    the first phrase. Complete the four-part texture, including in the second phrase a mod-
    ulation to B♭ and a borrowed iv⁶ chord. Label all chords and circle the roman numeral
    of the borrowed chord. Activate the texture with NCTs and/or arpeggiations.

F. Analyze the harmonies specified by the following figured bass and then make an
    arrangement for SATB chorus. This passage modulates.

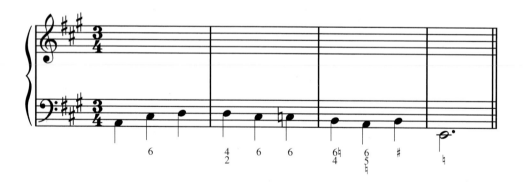

G. Arrange the first modulation below for SAB chorus and the second one for SATB chorus. Activate the textures with NCTs and/or arpeggiations. Arrange the metric and rhythmic structure so that the last chord comes on a strong beat. Label chords and NCTs.

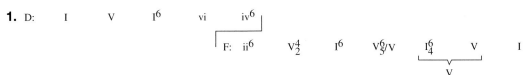

1. D: I   V   I⁶   vi   iv⁶

⌐ F: ii⁶   V⁴₂   I⁶   V⁶₅/V   I⁶₄   V   I

V

2. F: I   vii°⁶₅   I⁶   V⁶₅   I   vii°⁴₃/IV   iv⁶

⌐ b♭:   i⁶   iv   i⁶₄   V   i

V

H. Use the framework below as the basis for the beginning of a passage that starts in F major and modulates to D♭ major by means of mode mixture. Score for piano or for some combination of instruments in your class.

Chapter 22

THE NEAPOLITAN CHORD

EXERCISE 22-1

A. Label each chord. Include inversions, if appropriate.

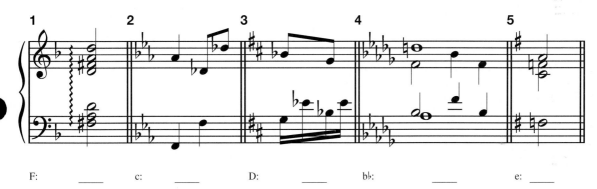

F: ____   c: ____   D: ____   b♭: ____   e: ____

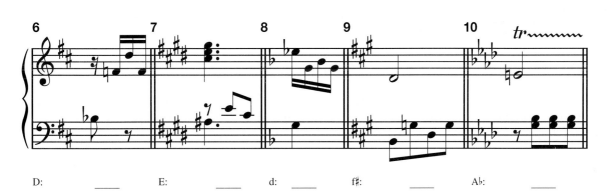

D: ____   E: ____   d: ____   f♯: ____   A♭: ____

B.   Notate each chord. Include key signatures.

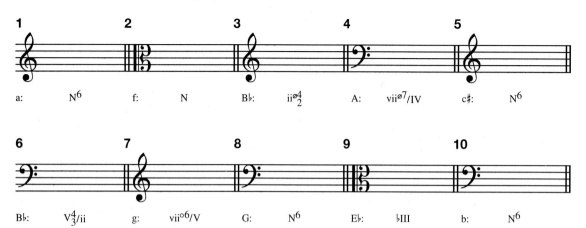

1

a: N⁶

2

f: N

3

Bb: ii⁰⁴₂

4

A: vii⁰⁷/IV

5

c#:   N⁶

6

Bb: V⁴₃/ii

7

g: vii°⁶/V

8

G: N⁶

9

Eb: bIII

10

b: N⁶

C.   Analysis.

   1.   Label chords and NCTs.

   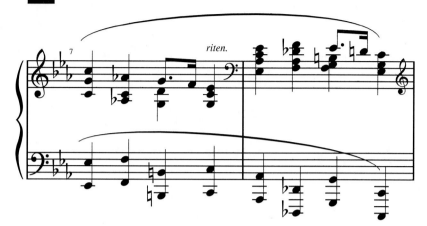   Chopin, Prelude Op. 28, No. 20

   2.   Label the chords in this excerpt.

   Beethoven, Sonata Op. 27, No. 2, I

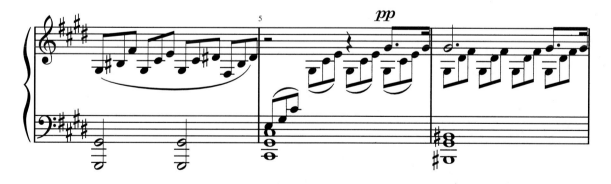

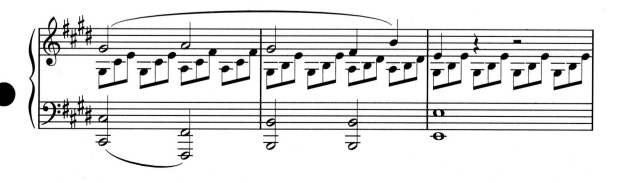

3. Label the chords in this excerpt. Where does the most unusual progression occur? (Don't let Beethoven's interesting use of $\hat{6}$ and $\hat{7}$ in mm. 1–3 confuse you—there is really just one chord in these three measures.)

Beethoven, Violin Sonata, Op. 47, II, Variation 3

4. This beautiful and moving theme illustrates the expressive power of the Neapolitan chord. Label all the chords and NCTs. The B♯ in m. 6 is not a chord tone but instead delays the arrival of C♯. By the time the C♯ arrives, however, the harmony has moved on. Does something similar happen in m. 8, or is the A♯ a chord tone? Be sure to listen to or play this example.

Mozart, Piano Concerto, K. 488, II

5. At this point in Schubert's famous "Erlkönig," the evil personality of the title character is finally expressed, with the help of the Neapolitan triad. Label the chords.

Schubert, "Erlkönig," Op. 1

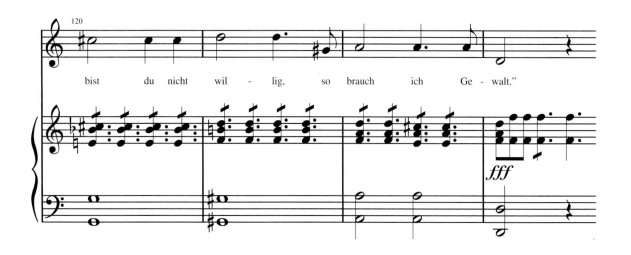

6. At the end of the song, the father's frantic ride comes to an end, and we hear the Neapolitan again. Label the chords.

Schubert, "Erlkönig," Op. 1

7. Mode mixture is involved in this excerpt in modulations to the key of the Neapolitan and back again. Label all chords, including common chords for both modulations.

Beethoven, Rondo, Op. 51, No. 1

D. For each exercise, provide the correct key signature and notate the specified chords
    preceding and following the N^6. Use the given three- or four-part texture in each case.

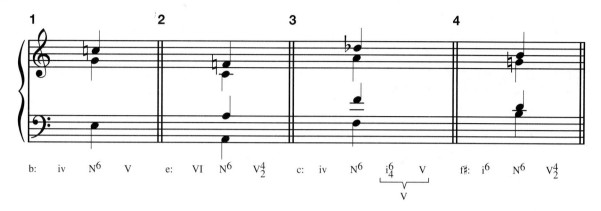

b: iv N^6 V   e: VI N^6 V^4_2 c: iv N^6 i^6_4 V   f#: i^6 N^6 V^4_2
                                                                            V

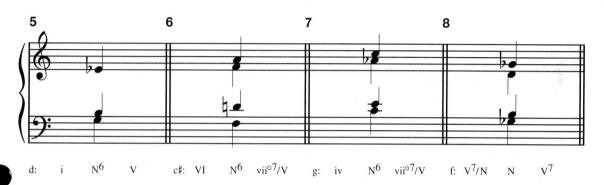

d: i N^6 V   c#:   VI N^6 $vii°^7/V$ g: iv N^6 $vii°^7/V$ f: V^7/N N V^7

E. Analyze the harmonies implied by the soprano/bass framework. Then fill in inner
    voices to make a four-part texture. Each exercise should contain a Neapolitan chord.

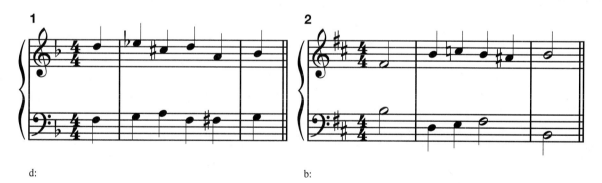

d: b:

3

c:

F. Analyze the chords specified by this figured bass and then make an arrangement for SATB chorus.

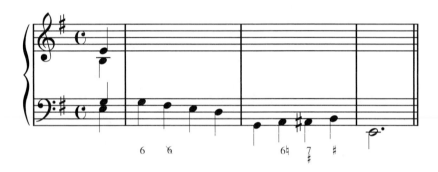

G. Make settings of the following progressions for three or four parts, as specified. Arrange the rhythmic/metric scheme so that the final chord of each progression comes on a strong beat. Activate the texture with arpeggiations and/or NCTs.

1. (4 parts) g: i   V   i^6 i   VI   V$^4_2$/N   N^6 vii^{o7}/V   i$^6_4$ V   i

V

2. (3 parts) e: i   V$^4_2$/iv   iv^6 i$^6_4$ N^6 V$^4_2$ i^6 vii^{o6} i

3. (4 parts) E♭:   I   I^6 vi   ii   V   I^6

d: N^6 vii^{o7}/V   i$^6_4$ V^7 i

V

4. (3 parts) b: i   V   VI   i^6 N^6

G: IV^6 V$^6_5$ I   V   I

H. Use the framework below as the first phrase of a three-phrase excerpt having the
    following structure:

Phrase 2 modulates to f♯ minor. Phrase 3 remains in f♯ minor and contains a
Neapolitan triad. After completing the framework, make a more elaborate version for
piano or for some combination of instruments in your class.

I. Make a setting of the following text or another text of your choice for three-part chorus. Include in your setting examples of the following:

Neapolitan triad

Mode mixture

Common-chord modulation

Your composition should begin and end in the same key. Be sure to include a harmonic analysis.

A storm of white petals,
Buds throwing open baby fists
Into hands of broad flowers.

—From "The Year," in *Cornhuskers* by Carl Sandburg, copyright 1918 by Holt, Rinehart and Winston, Inc.; renewed 1946 by Carl Sandburg. Reprinted by permission of Harcourt Brace & Company.

Chapter   23

AUGMENTED SIXTH CHORDS 1

EXERCISE 23-1

A. For each exercise below, provide the key signature, and then notate $\sharp\hat{4}$ to $\hat{5}$ on the top
    staff and $\hat{6}$ to $\hat{5}$ (or, in major, $\flat\hat{6}$ to $\hat{5}$) on the bottom staff. Finally, show an analysis of
    the implied chords as in the example.

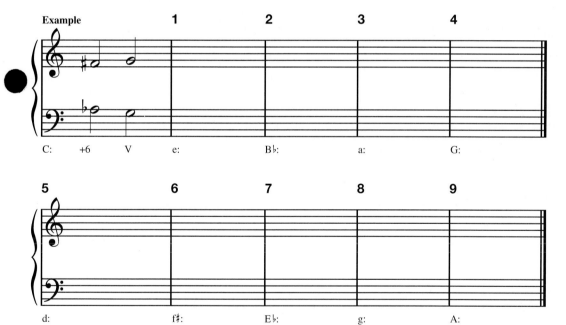

B. Label each chord, using inversion symbols where appropriate.

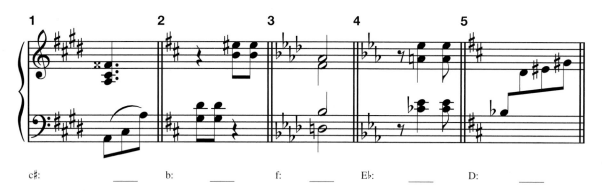

c#: _____   b: _____   f: _____   E♭: _____   D: _____

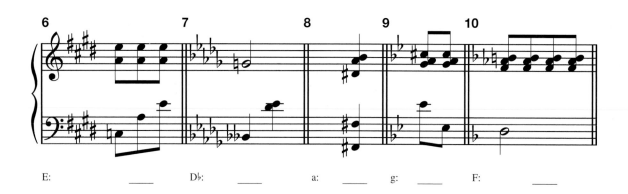

E: _____   D♭: _____   a: _____   g: _____   F: _____

C. Notate each chord in close position. Augmented sixth chords should be in their customary bass position ($\hat{6}$ in the bass in minor, ♭$\hat{6}$ in major). Include key signatures.

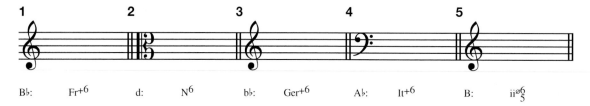

B♭:   Fr^{+6} d: N^6 b♭:   Ger^{+6} A♭:   It^{+6} B: ii$^{ø6}_5$

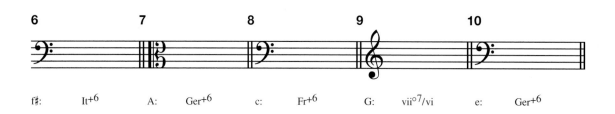

f#:   It^{+6} A: Ger^{+6} c: Fr^{+6} G: vii^{o7}/vi   e: Ger^{+6}

D. Label the chords in each example below. Also, discuss the details of the resolution of
    each augmented sixth chord. Do $\sharp\hat{4}$ and $\flat\hat{6}$ follow their expected resolutions to $\hat{5}$? How
    are parallel 5ths avoided in the Ger^{+6} resolution(s)?

1. Measures 2 to 5 of this excerpt are in d minor, although the key of VI (B♭) is strongly
    tonicized in mm. 2 to 3 (the second chord in m. 2 should be analyzed as a secondary
    function of VI). Common-chord modulations to two other keys occur in mm. 5 to 11.

Schumann, "Sehnsucht," Op. 51, No. 1

leuch - tet die Fer - ne mit gol - de-nem Licht, doch

hält mich der Nord, _____ ich er - rei - che sie nicht. O die

Schran - ken so eng, _____ und die Welt _____ so weit,

2. This excerpt begins and ends in g minor, but it contains modulations to two other keys (or tonicizations of two other chords). How do those keys relate to the "parent" tonality of g minor?

Schumann, "Die beiden Grenadiere," Op. 49, No. 1

Kind   zu Haus,   die   oh - ne mich   ver - der - ben."   "Was schert mich   Weib,

3. This very chromatic excerpt from an early Mozart string quartet contains an augmented sixth chord that resolves quite irregularly. Before you begin to label the chords, review the use of the subdominant chord in minor on pp. 64–65 and 243.

Mozart, String Quartet, K. 168, II (piano arrangement)

C:

4. This excerpt begins in C major and modulates. Where is there a 9-8 suspension?

Haydn, Quartet Op. 74, No. 3, II

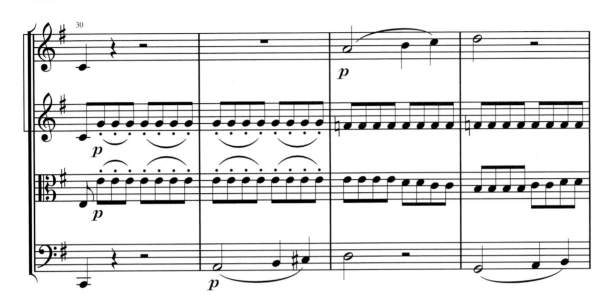

5. This excerpt modulates to the dominant, passing through another key on the way. The first chord in m. 8 is spelled enharmonically (imagine a G♮ instead of the F𝄪). Be sure to analyze a chord on beat 2 of m. 8.

Schumann, Tragödie, Op. 136, No. 3

6. The slow tempo of this theme allows some measures to contain several chords. In the first measure, for example, each bass note is harmonized by a new chord, with the exception of the B2. Discuss the various uses of the pitch class G♯/A♭ in this excerpt.

Beethoven, String Trio Op. 9, No. 3, II

E. Supply the missing voices for each fragment below. All are four-part textures.

g: ii°$_3^4$ It^{+6} V   F: IV^6 Ger^{+6} I$_4^6$ V   c: vii°$_2^4$ Fr^{+6} i$_4^6$ V
                                                    V   V

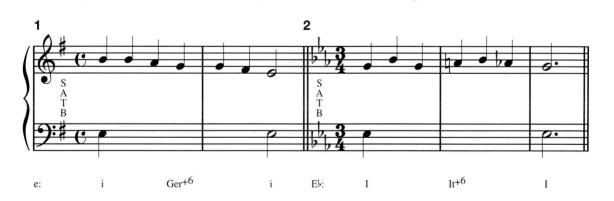

D: vi IV^6 Fr^{+6} V^7 I   b: ii°$_5^6$ (i$_4^6$) Ger^{+6} (i$_4^6$) V$_2^4$ i^6

F. Complete these harmonizations, adding one or two inner voices, as specified.

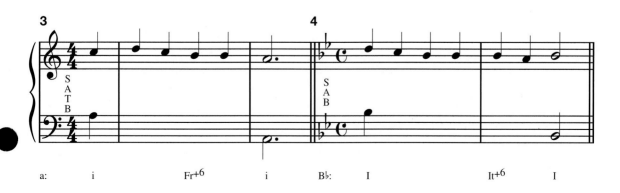

e: i Ger^{+6} i   E♭: I It^{+6} I

a: i Fr^{+6} i   B♭: I It^{+6} I

G. Analyze the harmonies specified by this figured bass and then make an arrangement
    for SATB chorus.

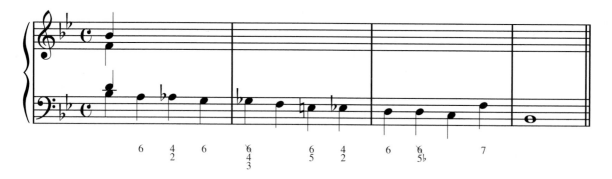

H. Analyze the harmonies implied by this soprano/bass framework, being sure to include
    an It⁺⁶. Then fill in the inner voices, following good voice-leading procedures. There
    are no NCTs in the bass and soprano lines.

I. Given below are mm. 1 to 2 of a four-measure phrase. Continue the passage to make
    a period (parallel or contrasting) that ends with a PAC in the key of the dominant.
    Include an augmented sixth chord.

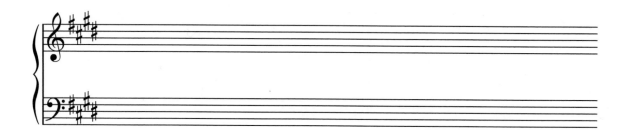

J. Make a setting of the following text or another text of your choice for three-part chorus. Include in your setting examples of the following:

Neapolitan triad

Mode mixture

Secondary function

Augmented sixth chord

Remember to include tempo indication and dynamic markings.

Two roads diverged in a wood, and I—
I took the one less traveled by,
And that has made all the difference.

—From "The Road Not Taken," by Robert Frost. From *The Poetry of Robert Frost,* edited by Edward Connery Lathem. Copyright 1916, © 1969 by Henry Holt and Company, Inc. Copyright 1944 by Robert Frost. Reprinted by permission of Henry Holt and Company, Inc.

Chapter 24

AUGMENTED SIXTH CHORDS 2

EXERCISE 24-1

A.   Label the chords in the keys indicated.

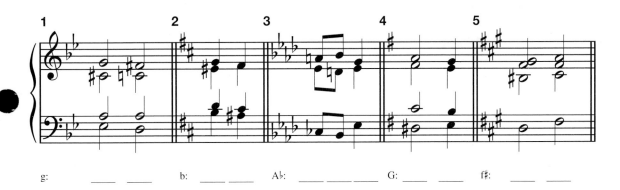

g: _____ _____   b: _____ _____   A♭: _____ _____   G: _____ _____   f♯: _____ _____

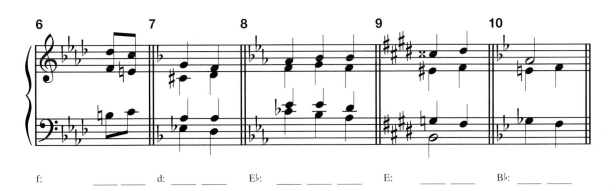

f: _____ _____   d: _____ _____   E♭: _____ _____   E: _____ _____   B♭: _____ _____

B.   Analysis.

1.   Label the chords in this example. Measures 10 to 12 could be analyzed in terms of secondary functions or as a modulation.

Tchaikovsky, "The Nurse's Tale," Op. 39, No. 19

2.   In a number of his works Scriabin used the chord found at the end of the first measure. Label the chords.

Scriabin, *Tragic Poem*, Op. 34

3. This excerpt will give you practice with both alto and tenor clefs. Label all chords and NCTs.

Schubert, String Trio D. 471

4. This example begins in A and modulates. Label the chords.

Schumann, "Novellette," Op. 21, No. 7 (simplified texture)

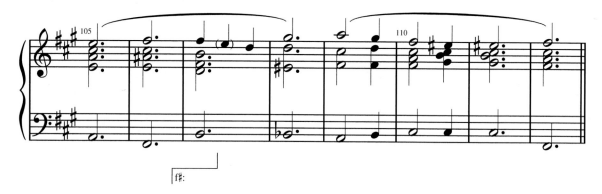

5. Label the chords.

Beethoven, Violin Sonata Op. 23, III

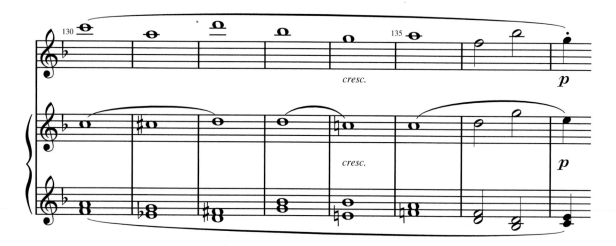

Chapter 25

ENHARMONIC SPELLINGS AND ENHARMONIC MODULATIONS

EXERCISE 25-1

A. Analyze the given chord. Then show any possible enharmonic reinterpretation(s) of
    that chord, keeping the same key signature. The enharmonic reinterpretation should
    involve a new key, not just an enharmonically equivalent key (like g♯ and a♭). Num-
    ber 1 is supplied as an example.

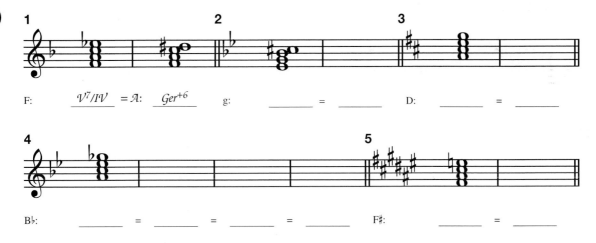

F: _V⁷/IV_ = A: _Ger⁺⁶_   g: _____ = _____   D: _____ = _____

B♭: _____ = _____ = _____ = _____   F♯: _____ = _____

B. Each of the following short passages contains an enharmonic modulation. Analyze
    each passage after playing it slowly at the piano and listening for the point of modu-
    lation. Do not try to analyze these passages without hearing them.

2

C. Analyze the progressions implied by these soprano and bass lines and fill in the inner voices. Analyze enharmonic common chords where indicated.

Use two different chords on the last beat of m. 2 and the first beat of m. 3 in Exercise 1.

D. Compose short passages similar to those in Part B. The given chord is to serve as the common chord in an enharmonic modulation. (Hint: As you sketch out your progression, notate the given chord first. Then find satisfactory ways to lead into and away from that chord.)

1. G to B. Common chord: V^7/IV in G.

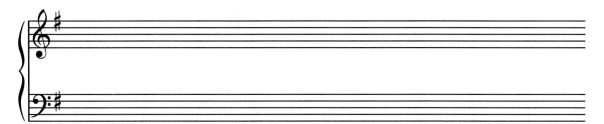

2. b to B♭. Common chord: vii°^{7}/iv in b.

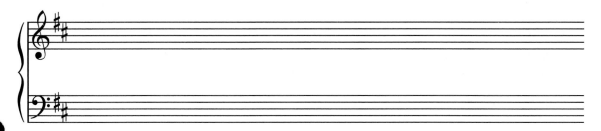

3. B♭ to E. Common chord: vii°$^6_5$ in B♭.

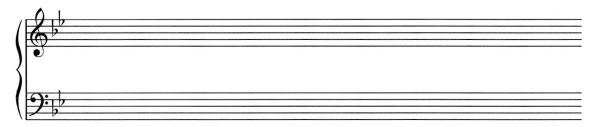

4. E to F. Common chord: Ger^{+6} in E.

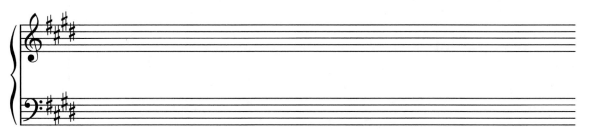

E.   Analysis. Be sure to play as much as you can of each excerpt.

1.   This passage modulates from f♯ minor to A♭ major by way of E major. The bass notes are found above the *"Ped."* markings—the other notes in the bass clef are arpeggiations into inner voices. Label all the chords, including common chords for both modulations.

Chopin, Nocturne Op. 27, No. 1

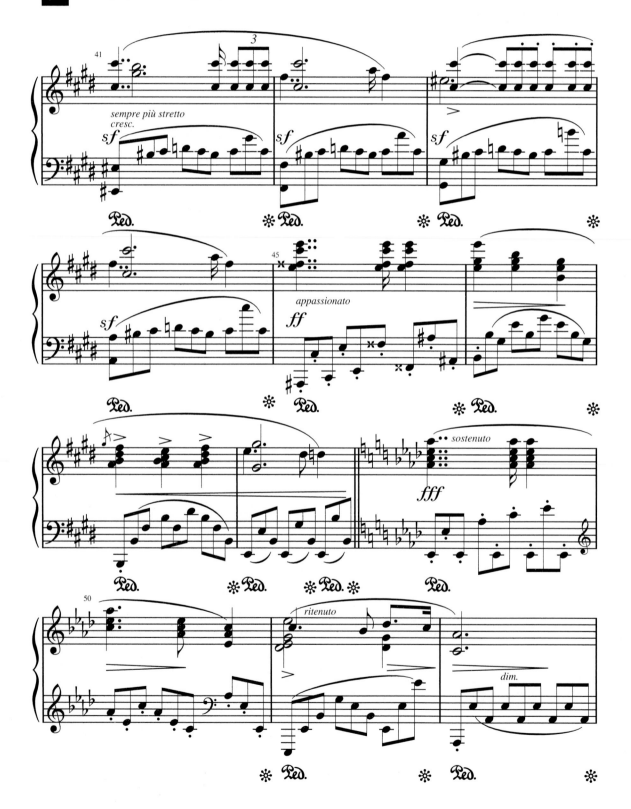

2. This excerpt begins in g minor. Label all the chords.

Beethoven, Sonata Op. 13, I

3. This excerpt is from the end of the exposition and the beginning of the development of a movement in sonata form (review pp. 332–334). The final cadence of the last B theme is shown in the first few measures of the excerpt (in E♭ major). The music then leads to a modulation to C minor in the first ending and to A minor in the second ending. Notice that the sonority first heard in m. 76 is used again twice, each time in a different way. (Bonus question: what *other* sonority in these measures is treated enharmonically?)

Brahms, Quartet, Op. 51, No. 1, I

4. The next excerpt is quite challenging. Label both chords and NCTs. You might find it helpful to label the chords with pop symbols before assigning roman numerals.

Haydn, Quartet Op. 76, No. 6, II

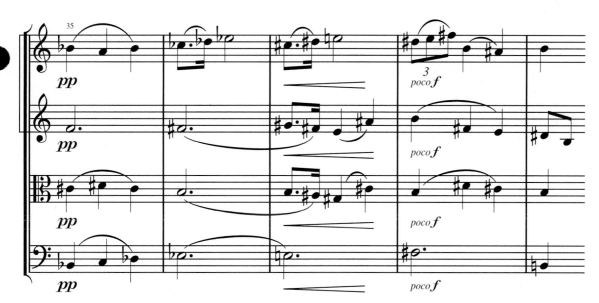

5. This dance modulates from D♭ to A and back again. Although both modulations involve enharmonicism, only one of them is a true enharmonic modulation—the other uses enharmonic spellings for convenience.

    a. Label all the chords, including two common-chord modulations.

    b. Label the enharmonic modulation.

    c. Name the form of this piece.

Schubert, Originaltänze, Op. 9 (D. 365), No. 14

F. Use mm. 31 to 34 of Part E, number 4, as the first phrase of an eight-measure parallel period. The second phrase should include an enharmonic modulation to a foreign key.

G. Compose the beginning of a song with piano accompaniment, using a text of your choice. Include two enharmonic modulations, one of them using a Ger^{+6} chord, the other a diminished seventh chord.

Chapter 26

FURTHER ELEMENTS OF
THE HARMONIC VOCABULARY

EXERCISE 26-1

A. In each fragment below, analyze the given chord. Then notate the specified chord in
    such a way that it leads smoothly into the given chord with acceptable voice leading.
    Some of the problems use a five-part texture for simpler voice leading.

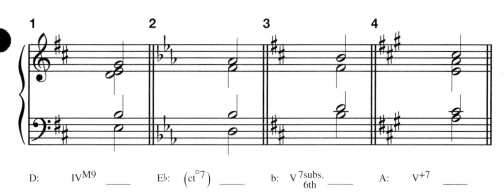

D: IV^{M9} ____   E♭: (ct$^{°7}$) ____   b: V$^{7subs.}_{6th}$ ____   A: V^{+7} ____

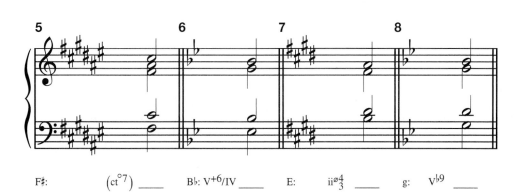

F♯:   (ct$^{°7}$) ____   B♭: V^{+6}/IV ____   E: ii$^{ø4}_{3}$ ____   g: V$^{♭9}$ ____

B. Compose four short passages for piano, each one making use of a different progression from Part A. The half-note durations do not need to be retained, but use the same voice leading.

C. Analysis. Throughout this section highlight (using arrows or whatever is convenient) any occurrences of the chords discussed in this chapter.

1. Label chords and NCTs.

Schumann, *Humoresque*, Op. 20

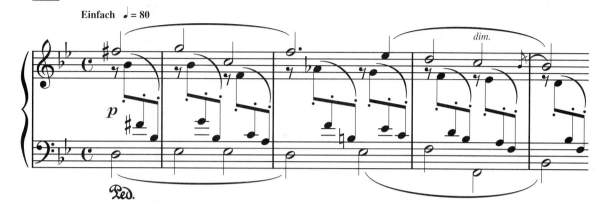

2. This excerpt features one of the chords discussed in the chapter. The last chord in m. 8 should be analyzed as a secondary function. What is the form of the excerpt?

Chopin, Nocturne, Op. 32, No. 2

3. a. Analyze this excerpt in f minor throughout. One of the chords is best analyzed as a chord with an added 6th.

b. Put parentheses around NCTs and be prepared to discuss them.

c. Diagram the phrase structure and label the form. Assume four-measure phrases.

Chopin, Mazurka, Op. 63, No. 2

4. The excerpt below is written for barbershop quartet. The treble clef part sounds an octave lower, and the melody is given to the second tenor (the bottom voice in the treble clef). Music for barbershop quartet frequently uses ct°7 chords, and you will find some in this excerpt, including one that embellishes a secondary dominant. Label all chords and NCTs, analyzing in A♭ throughout.

Ayer (arr. by Campbell), "Oh! You Beautiful Doll"

5. Harmonic sequences occupy most of this excerpt. Find the two sequences and bracket each occurrence of the sequential patterns. If it is possible to do so, label the chords in the sequences with roman numerals, perhaps in terms of shifting tonalities. Discuss briefly the large-scale harmonic/melodic function of each sequence. In other words, just what does each sequence accomplish harmonically and melodically?

Schumann, "Die Löwenbraut," Op. 31, No. 1

6. This familiar excerpt is easier to listen to than to analyze. The transpositions do not make the analysis any easier—clarinets in A and horns in F—nor do the four clefs in use. Do your best with the score (after all, conductors face this sort of problem every day), then check your work with the piano reduction that follows the excerpt.

Tchaikovsky, Symphony No. 6, Op. 74, I

7. The chord in m. 4 should be analyzed in two ways: the way in which we expect it to resolve when we first hear it and the way it actually functions.

Schubert, *Schwanengesang,* "Kriegers Ahnung"

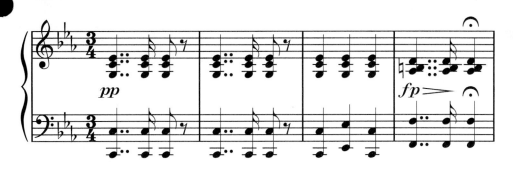

8. This excerpt ends with an enharmonic modulation leading to a cadence that implies the key of e, although it is not confirmed by the following phrase.

Schubert, String Quintet, I (piano reduction)

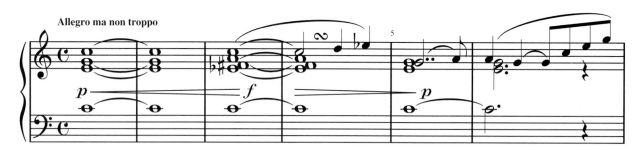

9. Label with roman numerals the two chords in this excerpt that are the most important structurally. The other chords are simultaneities connecting the structural chords. Label their roots. If any of these chords imply fleeting tonicizations, indicate this with roman numerals. The chord in m. 2 could be heard as a g triad with raised *and* lowered 5th (G–B♭–D♭–D♯) because the E♭ ascends chromatically to E, as we would expect D♯ to do. Find another chord in this passage that could be interpreted similarly.

Wagner, *Siegfried,* Act I (piano-vocal score)

10. In some ways this excerpt pushes traditional harmony toward its limits, especially through its disregard for conventional resolutions of dissonance. Nevertheless, the entire passage can be analyzed reasonably well in traditional terms. Label all the chords. Which portion of the excerpt is the most unconventional in terms of dissonance treatment?

Grieg, "The Mountain Maid," Op. 67, No. 2

Chapter 27

TONAL HARMONY IN THE LATE NINETEENTH CENTURY

EXERCISE 27-1

A. Examine the first twenty-five measures of the opening of *Tannhäuser*, given below, and do the following:

1. The opening eight measures show rather traditional harmonic function. Analyze these measures, using roman numerals (do all work on the music).

2. The following eight measures, which may also be analyzed with roman numerals, show less traditional harmonic movement. Cite at least three instances in which this is true (show measure number).

    a. _____

    b. _____

    c. _____

3. Analyze the sequence that begins at m. 17 and continues through m. 21.

    | | | | | |
    m. 17   m. 18   m. 19   m. 20   m. 21

    Use pop symbols, roman numerals, or a mixture of both, whichever seems appropriate. Circle those chords that are most strongly tonicized. How is such tonicization accomplished?

Wagner, *Tannhäuser*, Prelude to Act I (piano reduction)

B. Analyze the following chromatic sequences, then continue each as indicated.

Select one of the above sequence patterns to serve as the basis for a piano composition. You might want to create a melody over the background of block chords or perhaps modify the texture of the harmonies themselves. Nonessential or embellishing chords may be inserted within the sequence for the purpose of color.

C. Continue the following sequences as indicated. Then select one to serve as the harmonic basis for a piano or vocal composition in the style of one of the post-Romantic composers studied. Strive for contrapuntal interest and smooth voice leading.

D. Examine the following excerpt.

1. The opening key is designated as E major. What is interesting about the structure of the scale that forms the basis for mm. 2 and 3? _____

    _____

    _____

2. Provide roman numeral analysis for m. 2. _____
    In what way does the music in mm. 10 to 11 suggest more traditional treatment of tonality?

    _____

    _____

3. Describe the modulatory procedure that takes place in mm. 12 to 13. _____

    _____

    _____

4. Name the key introduced in m. 14. _____

    What is its relationship to the opening key? _____

5. Name two other keys hinted at between mm. 1 and 14. _____

    and _____ These keys represent what relationship to each other and to

    the opening key? _____

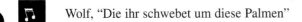

Wolf, "Die ihr schwebet um diese Palmen"

E.

1. Is there a clear tonal center in the opening five bars of the following excerpt? If so, what is it and how is it defined?_____

   _____

   _____

2. Using pop symbols, name the two sonorities found in mm. 6 and 7._____

   and _____ In what way could these chords be said to suggest functional harmony in the key of D major, which ultimately concludes the excerpt, as well as

   the piece? _____

   _____

3. What roman numerals are used in mm. 9 to 12 to prepare the cadence in D major?

   └─────────────┴─────────────┴─────────────┴─────────────┘
   m. 9   m. 10   m. 11   m. 12

Wolf, "Verschwiegene Liebe"

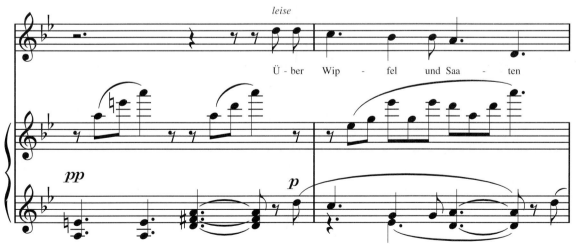

dan - ken sind frei.   Er -

F. The first ten measures of *Reverie* may be analyzed with traditional roman numerals
    (if you watch out for enharmonic respellings). Do so, then comment on reasons for
    the rather contemporary sound of the piece.

Payne, *Reverie*

_____

_____

_____

_____

_____

G.

1. The following excerpt begins and ends in E major. What is unusual about the manner in which the key is established in mm. 10 to 13?_____

_____

_____

2. Label on the music the harmonies found in mm. 14 to 22. Use pop symbols for your analysis.

3. What five-chord succession within mm. 14 to 22 represents an "omnibus" fragment?

_____

4. In what way is the approach to the closing E major harmony unusual? _____

_____

_____

5. By what means does Fauré make it convincing, nonetheless?

_____

_____

_____

Fauré, "Chanson d'Amour," Op. 27, No. 1 (mm. 10–22)

H.

1. In the *Siegfried* excerpt, analyze one essential harmony for each of the first eleven measures of the excerpt.

m. 1   m. 2   m. 3   m. 4   m. 5   m. 6   m. 7   m. 8   m. 9   m. 10   m. 11

2. Name at least three keys (including the first one) that are established throughout the course of this excerpt. Show the measure numbers.

_____   _____   _____

3. Show two instances in which modulation is effected by deceptive resolution, either of chords or of single pitches. Describe the process that takes place.

_____

_____

_____

Wagner, *Siegfried* (Act III, Scene 3)

I.

1. What is unusual about the treatment of tonality in the opening four measures of the
    Franck prelude? _____

    _____

    _____

2. Describe the nontraditional treatment of the dominant seventh sonority in mm. 5 to 9 of
    the excerpt. _____

    _____

    _____

3. In what way is the musical style significantly influenced by the treatment of nonhar-
    monic material? Consider both single tones and vertical sonorities. _____

    _____

    _____

    _____

Franck, *Prelude, Aria, and Finale for Piano* (Prelude)

J.   The following excerpt is taken from the *Barcarolle,* Op. 17, No. 6, by Richard Strauss (mm. 21–30).

    1.   What key is implied by the melody in the opening four bars? _____

    2.   What means does Strauss employ to negate that tonal implication and, indeed, any clear

        tonal implication? _____

        _____

        _____

        _____

    3.   Show the underlying harmonic structure of mm. 25 to 29, using pop symbols.

        m. 25   m. 26   m. 27   m. 28   m. 29

    4.   Within the passage shown above, locate and describe at least three examples of deceptive resolution that serve to make the chord succession convincing.

        a. _____

        b. _____

        c. _____

Strauss, *Barcarolle,* Op. 17, No. 6

Chapter 28

AN INTRODUCTION TO
TWENTIETH-CENTURY MUSIC

EXERCISE 28-1

A.   Add the appropriate accidentals to create the modal scale indicated:

C-Mixolydian   C-Dorian

C-Phrygian   C-Lydian

C-Aeolian   C-Locrian

B.   Add the appropriate accidentals to create the modal scale indicated:

D-Mixolydian   B-Dorian

F-Phrygian   G-Aeolian

E-Lydian   G-Locrian

C.   Answer the following questions about the diatonic modes:

   1.   The three modes that are essentially *major* in quality are the _____ ,

   _____ , and _____ modes.

   2.   The three modes that are essentially *minor* in quality are the _____ ,

   _____ , and _____ modes.

   3.   All the modes contain a perfect 5th from $\hat{1}$ up to $\hat{5}$ except the _____ mode.

   4.   The two modes that contain a leading tone are the _____ and

   _____ modes.

   5.   The two modes that contain a minor second from $\hat{1}$ up to $\hat{2}$ are the _____ and

   _____ modes.

   6.   The $\hat{1}$–$\hat{4}$ tetrachord in the Mixolydian mode matches that of the _____ mode.

   7.   Likewise, the opening tetrachords of the Aeolian and _____ modes are the

   same.

   8.   The four modes that contain a major 6th from $\hat{1}$ up to $\hat{6}$ are the _____ ,

   _____ , _____ , and _____ modes.

   9.   The three modes that contain a minor 6th from $\hat{1}$ up to $\hat{6}$ are the _____ ,

   _____ , and _____ modes.

   10.   Name the interval from $\hat{1}$ up to $\hat{4}$ in the Ionian mode. _____

   11.   Name the interval from $\hat{1}$ up to $\hat{4}$ in the Lydian mode. _____

   12.   Name the interval from $\hat{4}$ up to $\hat{7}$ in the Ionian mode. _____

   13.   Name the interval from $\hat{4}$ up to $\hat{7}$ in the Mixolydian mode. _____

D. Using a key signature (rather than appropriate accidentals), notate the following
modal scales in the clef indicated.

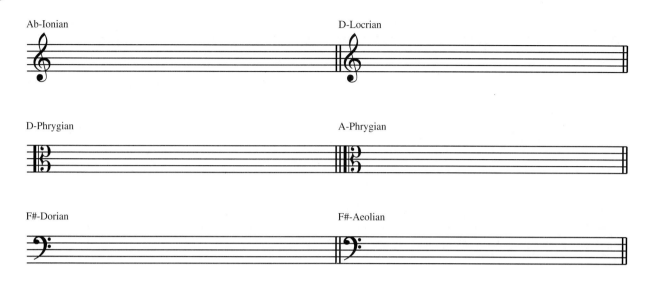

E. Notate the following pentatonic scales and hybrid modes starting on the pitch indicated.
Be sure to include the octave-related pitch.

F. Notate the following synthetic scales starting on the pitch indicated. Be sure to include the octave-related pitch.

G. Add the appropriate accidentals (or delete the appropriate notes) to create the scale indicated. You may choose a starting pitch of B or B♭.

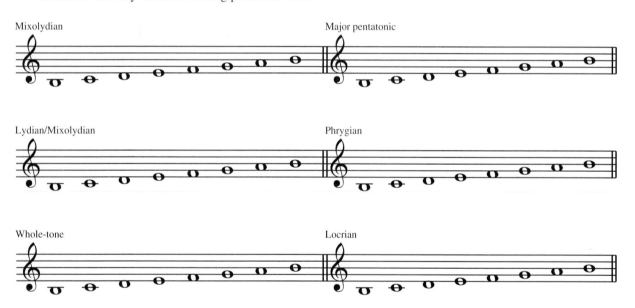

H.   Identify the scale used in the following passages.

1

_____

2   Allegretto

_____

3   Moderato

_____

4

_____

5

_____

6 **Moderately**

_____

I. Analysis. The following examples represent three versions of the principal tune from Debussy's "Fêtes." For each, identify the scale being used.

Debussy's "Fêtes," from *Nocturnes* (piano reduction)

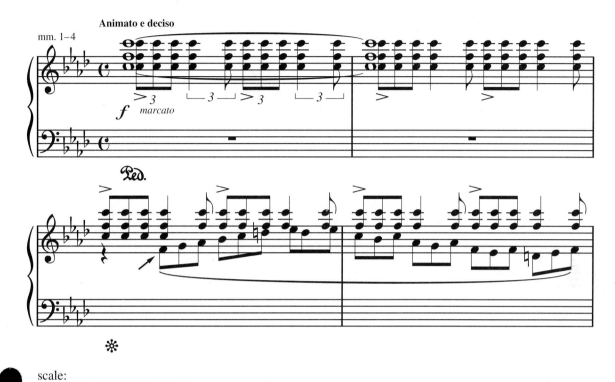

scale: _____

scale: _____

Used by permission of Edward B. Marks Music Co.

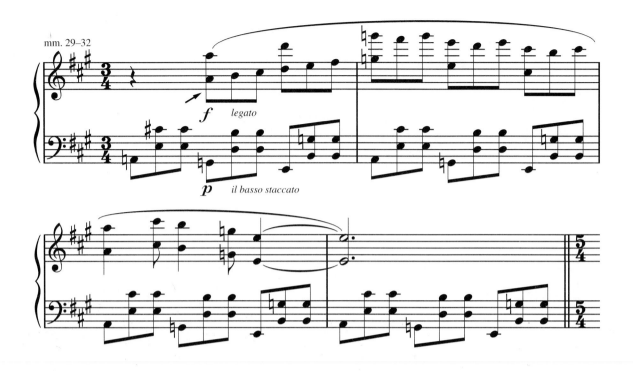

scale: _____

J.   Composition. Compose pieces according to the following specifications:

Using the major pentatonic scale B♭-C-D-F-G-B♭ as a basis, compose five brief melodies, each of which in turn establishes the indicated tone as a tone center. (Hint: D is tough. Why?)

1

2

3

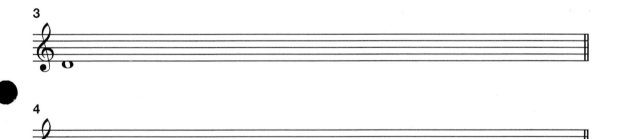

4

5

Create a melody based on the octatonic scale that emphasizes major and minor 3rds.
Carefully use rhythmic interest to create an exciting melody.

6

Create a two-voice composition based on a whole-tone scale. You might want to create
a symmetrical relationship between the two voices or perhaps treat them imitatively.
If your composition is for piano, experiment with the wide range of the keyboard.

7

EXERCISE 28-2

A. Describe the structure of the chords shown below by providing the correct symbol: use
    the symbol "Q" for quartal/quintal chords, "S" for secundal chords, and lead sheet
    symbols for tertian sonorities and polychords.

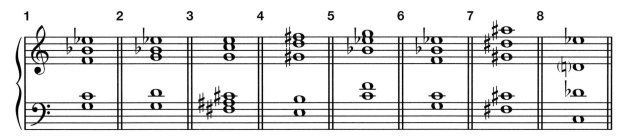

_____   _____   _____   _____   _____   _____   _____   _____

B. Identify the following sonorities as a quartal/quintal chord (Q), split-third chord,
    whole-tone chord, or tone cluster.

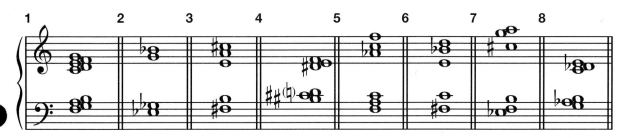

_____   _____   _____   _____   _____   _____   _____   _____

C. Describe the types of vertical sonorities found in the following examples as tertian, polychord, quartal, quintal, or added-note.

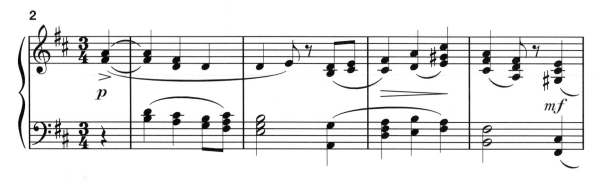

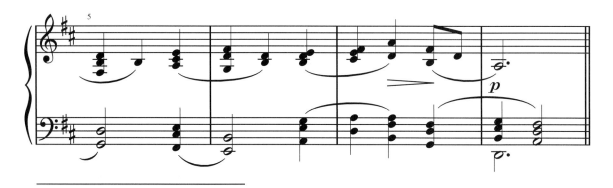

3

4

D. Complete the following passages using chromatic planing, or strict parallelism. That is, use the given initial sonority to create a passage where all voices move in the same direction by the same interval.

E. Complete the following passages using diatonic planing. That is, use the given initial
    sonority to create a passage where all voices move in the same direction by the same
    diatonic interval within the key signature indicated.

F. Complete the following passages, using the triad type indicated for each hand.
    Continue the scoring suggested by the first polychord, using the given outer parts con-
    sistently as either roots, 3rds, or 5ths of the sonority.

1 R.H. major, L.H. major

2 R.H. minor, L.H. minor

3 R.H. major, L.H. minor

4 R.H. major, L.H. minor

G. Analysis. Try to play or listen to the following example and answer the following questions:

  1. What technique is used to create form in this piano composition?

     _____

  2. Notate the scale that forms the basis of the opening *four* measures:

     Does the piece have a tone center? _____ If so, what is it? _____

     If you do not perceive one, why? _____

  3. What are the distinguishing characteristics of the opening two measures? _____

     _____

     _____

  4. In what ways is the character of the opening maintained throughout the piece?

     _____

     _____

  5. What is the derivation of the thematic gesture found in m. 3 of the right-hand part?

     _____ Locate three other instances in which that intervallic pattern appears (other than in the bass line).

     a. _____

     b. _____

     c. _____

Payne, *Arch*

H. Composition. Devise completions for the following passages. Include both black and white keys in your solution. Try to maintain stylistic consistency.

1

2

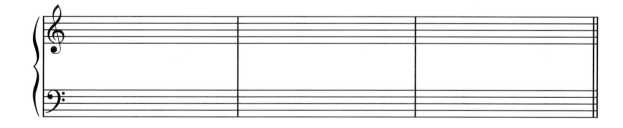

3

EXERCISE 28-3

A. Which of the following rhythmic procedures—added value, asymmetric meter, displaced accent, metric modulation, mixed meter, or non-retrogradable rhythm—are illustrated by the following examples:

1

_____

2

_____

3

_____

4

_____

5

_____

6

_____

B. Analysis. Comment on the rhythmic and metric devices employed in the following excerpts.

Stravinsky, "Danse de la foire," from *Petrouchka* (piano reduction)

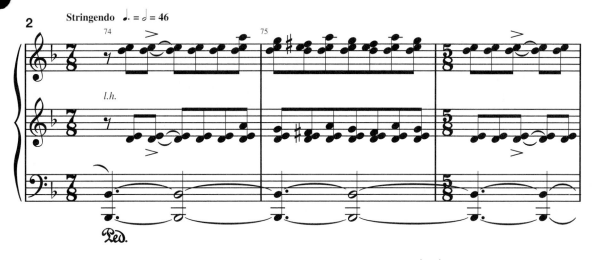

Used by permission of Edward B. Marks Music Co.

C. Composition. Compose a piece according to one of the following specifications:

  1. Create a polyrhythmic composition for two percussionists. Use any two like non-pitched percussion instruments (claves, cowbells, hand-claps, etc.).

  2. Create a composition for any two instruments that features a passage based on polymeter.

  3. Create a melody that utilizes two or more of the following rhythmic devices: added value, asymmetric meter, displaced accent, metric modulation, mixed meter, or non-retrogradable rhythm.

EXERCISE 28-4

A. First notate each pitch-class (pc) set on the staff provided (i.e., using *staff notation*).
Then determine each pc set's normal order and prime form. (Use the space indicated
on the staff as a workspace for your calculations.)

1 PC Set: (A,E,Eb)

STAFF NOTATION   WORKSPACE

2 PC Set: (D,A,F#)

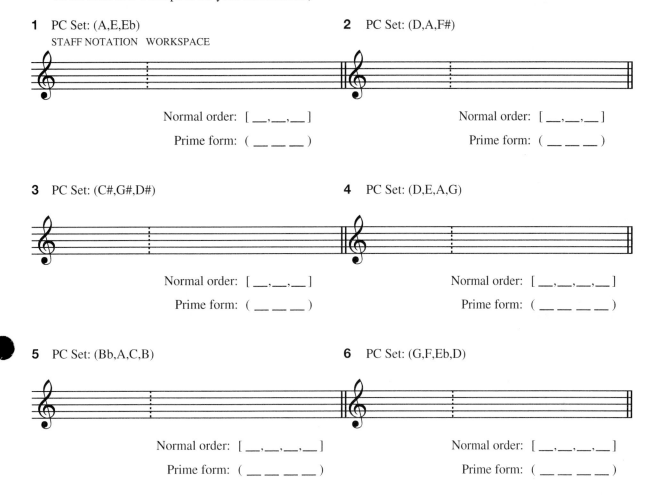

Normal order: [__,__,__]

Prime form: (__ __ __)

Normal order: [__,__,__]

Prime form: (__ __ __)

3 PC Set: (C#,G#,D#)

4 PC Set: (D,E,A,G)

Normal order: [__,__,__]

Prime form: (__ __ __)

Normal order: [__,__,__,__]

Prime form: (__ __ __ __)

5 PC Set: (Bb,A,C,B)

6 PC Set: (G,F,Eb,D)

Normal order: [__,__,__,__]

Prime form: (__ __ __ __)

Normal order: [__,__,__,__]

Prime form: (__ __ __ __)

B. For each of the following sonorities (trichords and tetrachords), provide the normal
    order, prime form, Forte name and interval class (ic) vector.

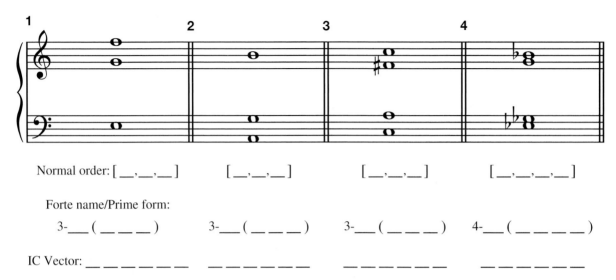

Normal order: [__,__,__]   [__,__,__]   [__,__,__]   [__,__,__,__]

Forte name/Prime form:

3-___ (___ ___ ___)   3-___ (___ ___ ___)   3-___ (___ ___ ___)   4-___ (___ ___ ___ ___)

IC Vector: __ __ __ __ __ __   __ __ __ __ __ __   __ __ __ __ __ __   __ __ __ __ __ __

Normal order: [__,__,__,__]   [__,__,__,__]   [__,__,__,__]   [__,__,__,__]

Forte name/Prime form:

4-___ (___ ___ ___ ___)   4-___ (___ ___ ___ ___)   4-___ (___ ___ ___ ___)   4-___ (___ ___ ___ ___)

IC Vector: __ __ __ __ __ __   __ __ __ __ __ __   __ __ __ __ __ __   __ __ __ __ __ __

C. Analysis. *from ritual to romance* for solo piano by Reginald Bain, 1st movement, mm. 1–8, which follows, opens with an atonal passage. Try to play the example and then answer the following questions:

1. Determine the normal order of the initial four-note melodic gesture (C,C♯,G,F♯). To what set class does this pc set belong?

    Normal order: [__, __, __, __] Belongs to set class: 4-__ (__ __ __ __)

2. Find two other melodic instances of this set class in the passage. Circle these occurrences on the score and mark them with the appropriate Forte name.

3. The three-note melodic cell (G,F♯,B♭) plays an important role in this introductory passage. Determine this pitch-class set's normal order. To what set class does it belong?

    Normal order: [__, __, __] Belongs to set class: 3-__ (__ __ __)

4. Find four instances of this set class in m. 6. Circle them on the score and mark them with the appropriate Forte name.

5. Determine the normal order of the chord (B,E,B♭) in the right hand, m. 2. To what set class does this pc set belong?

    Normal order: [__, __, __] Belongs to set class: 3-__ (__ __ __)

6. Find another instance of this set class in the right hand. Circle it on the score and mark it with the appropriate Forte name.

7. To what interval class does the left hand gesture in m. 2 belong?

    ic___

    Is this interval class prominently featured in the set classes you identified above?

    Yes/No (circle one)

8. A new set class begins to play an important role in m. 5. Two occurrences may be found in the right hand melody, mm. 5–6. What set class is it?

    Set class: 3-__ (__ __ __)

    In the melody mm. 5–6, circle both occurrences and mark them with the appropriate Forte name.

Bain, *from ritual to romance,* 1st movement, mm. 1–8

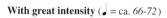

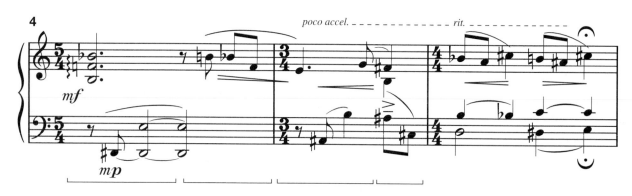

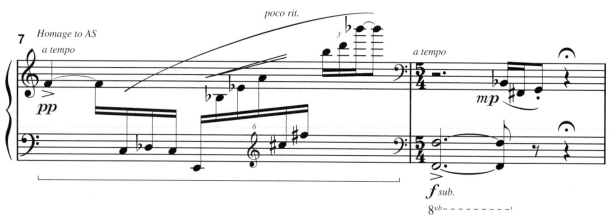

D. Composition. Compose a piece according to one of the following specifications:

   1. Create a melody that begins with a statement of set class 3-1 (012) and goes on to emphasize the following interval classes: ic2 (e.g., M2 or m7), ic1 (e.g., m2 or M7) and ic5 (e.g., P4 or P5).

   2. Create a composition for piano that is based on two harmonic cells and two melodic cells. For example, you might choose set classes 3-9 (027) and 3-7 (025) for your harmonic cells and ic1 and ic2 for your melodic cells.

EXERCISE 28-5

A. The series given below forms the basis for Berg's *Lyric Suite*. Notate the I_0 form on the staff provided, then complete the 12×12 matrix. Label the series forms using the blanks provided.

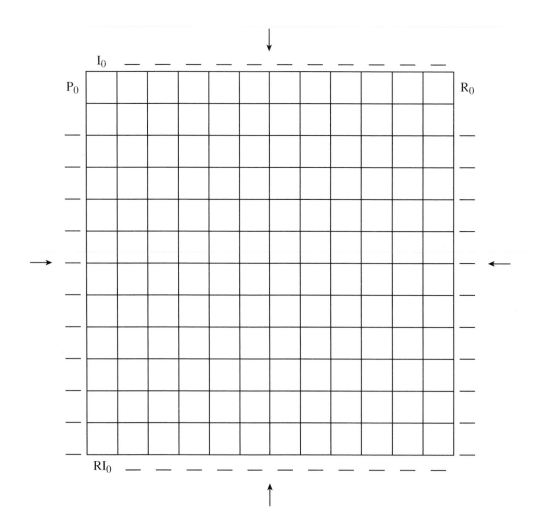

B. Answer the following questions about the series from Berg's *Lyric Suite*.

1. In the following trichordal segmentation of the series, identify the set class to which each
    discrete trichord belongs by providing its Forte name and prime form.

3-__ (__ __ __)   3-__ (__ __ __)   3-__ (__ __ __)   3-__ (__ __ __)

2. In the following tetrachordal segmentation of the series, identify the set class to which each
    discrete tetrachord belongs by providing its Forte name and prime form.

4-__ (__ __ __ __)   4-__ (__ __ __ __)   4-__ (__ __ __ __)

3. Determine the normal order of the two discrete hexachords.

                    1st Hexachord   2nd Hexachord

    Normal order: [__, __, __, __, __, __]   [__, __, __, __, __, __]

    From what scale do the two hexachords appear to be derived? The _____ scale.

4. Examine the intervallic structure of the series by filling in the blanks to indicate the number
    of semitones up to the next pitch class. For example, F-E is up 11 semitones.

    <u>11</u>   __   __   __   __   __   __   __   __   __   __

    What is interesting about the intervallic structure of this series? _____

    _____

C.

1. Notate the I_8 and R_3 series forms on the staves provided. The first note has been done for you.

P_0

I_8

R_3

2. Mirror (invert) the intervals.   **3.** Transpose a m3 higher.

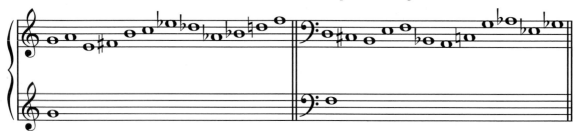

4. Transpose the retrograde a P4 higher.   **5.** Mirror (invert) the retrograde.

6. Which of the above is not a twelve-tone series? _____

D. Analysis

1. "Full Moon" by Otto Joachim is based on a 12-tone series. It employs a single series form that we will call P_0. First, identify the series and notate it (using the treble clef) on the staff provided below. (Hint: The series is presented for the first time in mm. 1-3. The order of the pitch classes in m. 3 is Eb-Bb-Gb-Db.)

P_0

Order

numbers: 1   2   3   4   5   6   7   8   9   10   11   12

Now trace the presentation of the series in mm. 1-24 by marking series forms (remember, the piece only employs P_0) and order numbers (1–12) on the score.

from *Twelve 12-Tone Pieces for Children*
© Copyright 1961 by BMI Canada Ltd. Copyright assigned 1969 to Berandol Music Ltd. Scarborough.

In some ways, "Full Moon" sounds almost impressionistic. What compositional devices has the composer employed to create this effect?

_____

_____

_____

2. "The Moon Rises" by Ernst Krenek is based on the following 12-tone series:

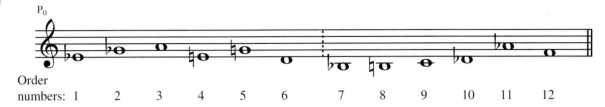

Order
numbers: 1   2   3   4   5   6   7   8   9   10   11   12

Like Joachim's "Full Moon," it employs a single series form (P_0). Trace the presentation of the series throughout the course of the piece by marking order numbers (1–12) on the score.

Krenek, "The Moon Rises," from *Twelve Short Piano Pieces,* Op. 83

"The Moon Rises" from *Twelve Short Piano Pieces* by Ernst Krenek. Copyright © 1939 (renewed) by Associated Music Publishers, Inc. (BMI). International copyright secured. All rights reserved. Reprinted by permission.

3. "Glass Figures" by Ernst Krenek, is based on the following 12-tone series. In preparation for the work that follows, notate the I_0 and R_0 forms of the series on the staves provided:

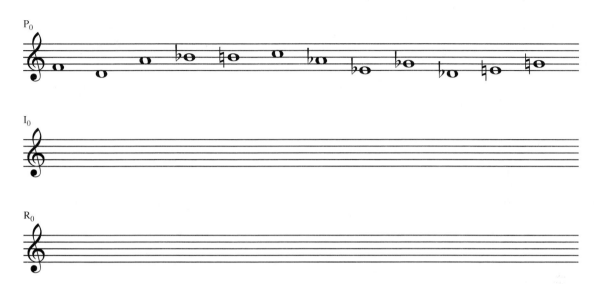

In examining the music, you will note that the first measure of the right hand opens with the first three notes of I_0, whereas the left hand features the first two notes of R_0. The third note of this latter series form D♭, is accommodated by the right hand because the third note of I_0 is also a D♭. Following this, the roles of the series forms are reversed, with the left hand picking up I_0 while the right hand continues with R_0. Because of the frequency of this type of exchange where two or more series forms are involved, it is advisable to use different-colored pencils to indicate different series forms in operation.

Krenek, "Glass Figures," from *Twelve Short Piano Pieces,* Op. 83

E.   Composition. Using the series for "The Moon Rises" shown below, compose a two-voice composition, the upper voice of which is based on a transposed series form while the lower voice makes use of a retrograde series form. You might want to try using instruments other than piano, such as violin and cello or two flutes.

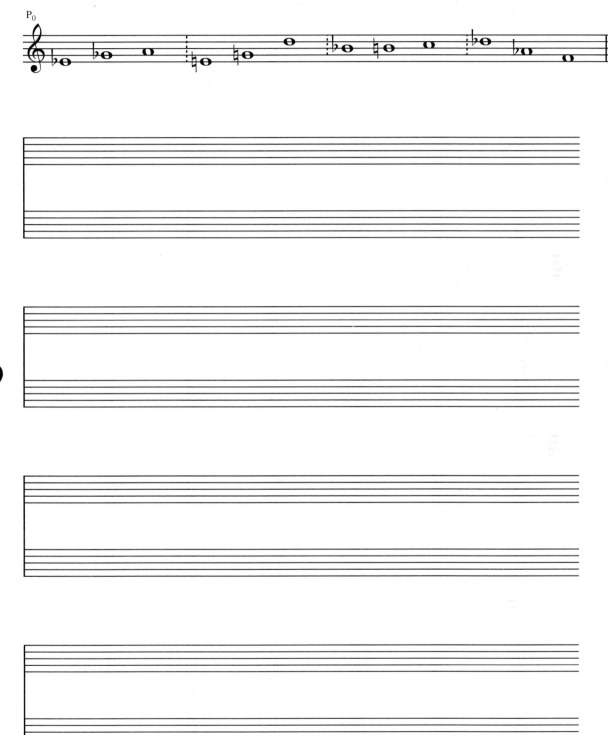

EXERCISE 28-6

A. With the help of your instructor, find works that illustrate the principles of aleatory or chance, minimalism, the use of texture and expanded instrumental resources, and electronic music discussed in Chapter 28. Then try the following exercises.

   1. Compose a short piece featuring aleatoric or indeterminate elements. Prepare a performance for class.

   2. Analyze and write a summary of a piece that combines live performer and recorded music. On the basis of your findings, compose a piece in this style.

   3. Compose a piece featuring special effects for your instrument or voice. Perform the piece in class.

   4. Compose a one measure melodic gesture (theme) that will form the basis for a minimalist piece. Your composition should be based entirely on rhythmic modifications of this theme. Have the piece performed in class. Be sure that your performance directions are perfectly clear. (Hint: Your class performance will go much better if you arrange at least a brief rehearsal first!)

Compact Discs to Accompany Workbook

THE PERFORMERS

Jana Holzmeier, *soprano*
Jennifer Murray, *soprano*
Julia Armstrong, *mezzo-soprano*
Tim Campbell, *tenor*
David L. Jones, *tenor*
David Stevens, *tenor*
Joel Quade, *baritone*
Richard Womack, *baritone*
Elizabeth Whitten, *flute*
David Pinkard, *bassoon*
Michael Misner, *horn*
James Wester, *horn*
Jennifer Bourianoff, *violin*
Marian Mentel, *violin*
Roger Graybill, *organ*
Jeff Hellmer, *piano (popular and jazz)*
Myra Spector, *jazz vocals*
David Mead, Alejandro Hernandez-Valdez, *piano and harpsichord*
Kyle Sigrest, *piano II*

The Barton Strings
Beth Blackerby, *violin*
Jennifer Bourianoff, *violin and viola*
Martha Carapetyan, Bruce Williams, *viola*
Carolyn Blubaugh-Hagler, *violoncello*

Tosca String Quartet
Leigh Mahoney, *1st violin*
Tracy Seeger, *2nd violin*
Ames Asbell, *viola*
Sara Nelson, *cello*

Chamber Choir—David Mead, *conductor*
Judith Kanana, Carol Hopkins, *soprano*
Brooke Lehr, Kellie McCurdy, *contralto*
Oliver Worthington, *tenor*
Te Oti Rakena, Steven Olivares, *bass*

Orchestra—David Mead, Alejandro Hernandez Valdez, *conductors*
Elizabeth Whitten, Michelle Clover Neal, *flute*
Pamela Whitcomb, Lana Neal, *oboe*
Marisa Bannworth Wester, Shannon Thompson, *clarinet*
David Pinkard, Rhonda Collison, *bassoon*
James Wester, Michael Misner, Richard Wheatley, Kellie Babcock, *horn*
Thomas Caswell, Stephen Miles, *trumpet*
Sean Scot Reed, David Garcia, David Hendricksen, *trombone*
Richard Short, *timpani*
Marian Mentel, *concertmaster*; Tera Shimizu, *principal violin II*
Jennifer Fedie, Wei He, Daniel McAtee, Sean Milligan, Hye-Sung Oh, Sue-Jean Park, Linda Piatt, Thomas Sender, Marvin Suson, Alicija Usarek, *violin*
Joseph Tan, Mark Sattler, Jason Elinoff, *viola*
Paul Rhodes, Kirsten Eggen, Sara Nelson, Victorial Wolff, *violoncello*
John Rosenkrans, Robert Jenkins, *contrabass*

Mark Ellis, *announcer*
David Mead, *producer*
Andrew Murphy, Frank Simon, *engineers*
J. Burke Hunn, Michael Czysz, *assistant engineers*

Recorded at the School of Music, University of Texas at Austin

Listening Example track information on next page.

LISTENING EXAMPLES

CD 1

Disc Duration:
45:13:14

Track	Name
1	WB 3-3 C
2	WB 3-4 B1
3	WB 3-4 B2
4	WB 3-4 B3
5	WB 4-1 C1
6	WB 4-1 C2
7	WB 4-2 C1
8	WB 4-2 C2
9	WB 5-2 A
10	WB 5-3 A
11	WB 7-1 C1
12	WB 7-1 C2
13	WB 8-1 A1
14	WB 8-1 A2
15	WB 8-1 A3
16	WB 9-1 A1
17	WB 9-1 A2
18	WB 9-1 A3
19	WB 9-1 A4
20	WB 9-1 A5
21	WB 9-1 A6
22	WB 10-1 B1
23	WB 10-1 B2
24	WB 10-1 B3
25	WB 10-1 B4
26	WB 10-1 B5
27	WB 10-1 B6
28	WB 10-1 B7
29	WB 11-1 A2
30	WB 12-1 A4
31	WB 12-1 A5
32	WB 12-1 A6
33	WB 13-1 B
34	WB 13-2 B1
35	WB 13-2 B2
36	WB 13-2 B3
37	WB 13-2 B4
38	WB 14-1 C1
39	WB 14-1 C2
40	WB 14-1 C3
41	WB 14-1 C4
42	WB 14-1 C5
43	WB 15-1 C1
44	WB 15-1 C2
45	WB 15-1 C3
46	WB 15-1 C4
47	WB 15-1 F
48	WB 16-2 A1
49	WB 16-2 A2
50	WB 16-2 A3
51	WB 16-2 A4
52	WB 16-2 A5
53	WB 16-2 A6
54	WB 17-2 A1
55	WB 17-2 A2
56	WB 17-2 A3
57	WB 17-2 A4
58	WB 17-2 A5
59	WB 18-2 A1
60	WB 18-2 A2
61	WB 18-2 A3
62	WB 18-2 A4
63	WB 18-2 A5
64	WB 18-2 A6
65	WB 18-2 A7
66	WB 18-2 A8
67	WB 19-1 A1
68	WB 19-1 A2
69	WB 19-1 A3
70	WB 19-1 A4
71	WB 19-1 A5
72	WB 20-1 A
73	WB 20-1 B
74	WB 20-1 C
75	WB 20-1 D
76	WB 20-1 E

CD 2

Disc Duration:
40:09:08

Track	Name
1	WB 21-1 C1
2	WB 21-1 C2
3	WB 21-1 C3
4	WB 21-1 C4
5	WB 21-1 C5
6	WB 21-1 C6
7	WB 22-1 C1
8	WB 22-1 C2
9	WB 22-1 C3
10	WB 22-1 C4
11	WB 22-1 C5
12	WB 22-1 C6
13	WB 22-1 C7
14	WB 23-1 D1
15	WB 23-1 D2
16	WB 23-1 D3
17	WB 23-1 D4
18	WB 23-1 D5
19	WB 23-1 D6
20	WB 24-1 B1
21	WB 24-1 B2
22	WB 24-1 B3
23	WB 24-1 B4
24	WB 24-1 B5
25	WB 25-1 E1
26	WB 25-1 E2
27	WB 25-1 E3
28	WB 25-1 E4
29	WB 25-1 E5
30	WB 26-1 C1
31	WB 26-1 C2
32	WB 26-1 C3
33	WB 26-1 C5
34	WB 26-1 C6
35	WB 26-1 C7
36	WB 26-1 C8
37	WB 26-1 C9
38	WB 26-1 C10
39	WB 27-1 A
40	WB 27-1 D
41	WB 27-1 E
42	WB 27-1 F
43	WB 27-1 G
44	WB 27-1 H
45	WB 27-1 I
46	WB 27-1 J
47	WB 28-1 H2
48	WB 28-1 H3
49	WB 28-1 H4
50	WB 28-2 C1
51	WB 28-2 C2
52	WB 28-2 C3
53	WB 28-2 C4
54	WB 28-2 G
55	WB 28-3 B1